A Book for All S

Poems, Lessons and Activities for 70 Special Days

by
Greta Barclay Lipson, Ed.D.

illustrated by Susan Kropa

Cover by Susan Kropa

Copyright © Good Apple, Inc., 1990

ISBN No. 0-86653-540-3

Printing No. 98765432

Good Apple, Inc.
1204 Buchanan St., Box 299
Carthage, IL 62321-0299

Dedication

A book for all seasons and special days is a natural metaphor for enduring friendship. And so this book is dedicated to Jack and Bea Canchester—the J.C.'s—with whom we have shared a precious bond over these many warm and wonderful years. "How many things by season season'd are—to their right praise and true perfection."

GA1153

Acknowledgement

From my heart to yours, Billy D. and Ger. I thank you a zillion times—and you know why!

iii

GA1153

Table of Contents

GA1153

GA1153

GA1153

GA1153

Introduction

It is a great treat to know that throughout the year, with each season and every month, there are special event days that spice the instructional day and relieve the mundane.

Here is a collection of seventy seasonal poems for young people, with corresponding background information and suggested activities. The month-by-month table of contents reveals the spread of events which provide perennial and dependable learning concepts throughout the school year. These lessons are interdisciplinary in scope and may be used to inspire serendipitous ideas across the curriculum.

You may choose to squeeze the July and August lessons into your conventional school year because National Hot Dog Month, Joe Miller Joke Day, and Hug an Ump Day are too good to miss!

Make use of the poems and illustrations with an opaque projector for a school year's worth of bulletin boards. Use parts of poems if that works best for you. Modify the ideas up or down the age group scale. Adapt everything here to suit your objectives—which is the best rule of thumb for all materials at any time. Remember—a suggestion in a book of this kind is only the stimulus for innovation and is not written in stone.

The format of the book allows students to savor the language in whichever mode they prefer to express themselves. Each "special day" features a three-part lesson plan which helps structure discussion, writing and exploratory thinking. When the teacher reads the poetry aloud, it becomes an experience in which all the students can share—from the least able reader to the best. Another choice is to duplicate the poems as handouts for individual commentary.

The special days presented here offer a variety of moods from serious to humorous (see Whiner's Day in December). These days may have been established by Congress, by presidential proclamation, by tradition, religion, by ethnic groups, seasons, or by a madcap regional inspiration.

As a bonus, students may designate their own special days using the format of the book to express their own personal interests which may be earnest or tongue-in-cheek. An examination of any book of special event days illustrates that there is no limit to the popular imagination and the things people are prepared to celebrate.

Reproducible calendars of "Coming Events" on pages 142-147 may be used for student information.

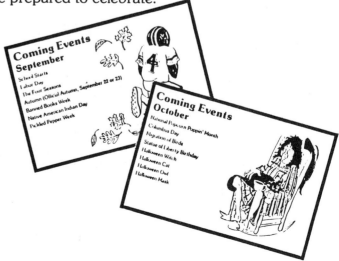

1

Lesson 1: School Starts

The start of school is an anxious, yet hopeful time for students who have countless concerns about what the year may hold for them. Many of them sincerely feel that the fresh start augurs good things for the future and that the new term will be the very best ever. It is this affirmative view that teachers want to support and hope to sustain by establishing a sound learning environment. A warm sense of community, belonging and caring is a human investment that pays dividends in the classroom.

Activities

1. In the first week of school you have listened to a variety of introductory remarks from your teachers. Discuss the following questions written on the board. Write your personal reactions.

   a. What have you heard enough of today?
   b. Of all the things you have heard, what do you think was good? What was bad? What was confusing?
   c. What have you been thinking during the teacher's introductions?

2. As a student, you need answers to many *operational* questions at the start of a semester. Besides—everybody appreciates accurate school information about the new term. With the help of your teacher, make an information bulletin, organized for quick reading, which includes staff and teacher names (correctly spelled), school phone numbers, and other relevant details of your choice.

3. Teachers may post their own "Rules of the Management." Rule 1: The teacher is always right. Rule 2: In all situations remember Rule 1. (A little humor is good for the soul.)

1. School Starts

Back to School

Are the teachers fair?
Will they understand
That the work I do
Is the best I can?

Will the kids like me?
Will they think I'm smart?
Will I find some friends
From the very start?

Will the days be hard?
Will the marks be tough?
Can I see things through,
When the work gets rough?

If you want the truth,
About how I feel,
I have to admit
That my fear is real.

Greta B. Lipson

GA1153

Lesson 2: Labor Day

Labor Day honors the struggles and achievements of all working people in America. It falls on the first Monday in September and has come to signal the official end of summer. It is traditionally a day of festive gatherings for families and friends. In 1882 two men introduced the concept of Labor Day: Matthew Maguire, a machinist from Paterson, New Jersey, and Peter J. McGuire, a carpenter from New York City. McGuire, who founded both the Knights of Labor and The United Brotherhood of Carpenters and Joiners, envisioned the celebration as being only a labor union event. It became a national holiday when President Grover Cleveland signed a bill on June 28, 1894, twelve years after the first Labor Day parade. Labor Day is a time to think about the respectability of work and the profoundly important role of the worker.

Activities

1. When families move into an area they need goods, services, and institutions to provide them with the necessities of life. What categories and occupations are essential to a community? Brainstorm the lists on the chalkboard. How inclusive and long will the lists be? (Start with schools, hospitals, police and fire protection, banks, churches, supermarkets, gas stations, restaurants, appliance and clothing stores.)

2. Research occupations in the present and choose one to study in detail. Organize a presentation of careers in which each person responds to questions about the training, salary, and aptitudes that are part of that occupation. Research unusual occupations for discussion. A projection of future occupations based upon current technology is another flight into fantasy which could become reality. Which fields of employment were not around twenty, thirty or fifty years ago? (Computers, robotics, space flight, electronic music . . .)

GA1153

2. Labor Day

Labor Day Rites

Hey you! Working person!
Didn't you say this was Labor Day?
Then why aren't you laboring?

You mean we don't labor?
You mean we all go out
And have a parade instead?

Now I understand.

Hey you!
Get out there and march—
On a day that celebrates working
    and workers.

Give a speech!
Attend a rally!
Make a picnic!
Have a good old family time!

But whatever you do—
Be sure not to labor on Labor Day.

Greta B. Lipson

Lesson 3: The Four Seasons

Whichever is your favorite season, it is a time for celebration when the first day of that season arrives. It is a pleasure to mark the calendar accordingly. Here are the first days of the four seasons:

Spring: March 20 or 21, vernal equinox (equal days and nights)
Summer: June 20 or 21, summer solstice (the longest day of the year)
Fall: September 22 or 23, autumnal equinox (equal days and nights)
Winter: December 21 or 22, winter solstice (the shortest day of the year)

The seasons are differentiated by temperature, weather, hours of daylight and the things that grow during that time. The seasons are caused by the tilt in the earth's axis as it revolves around the sun. In summer, the Northern Hemisphere is tipped toward the sun, receiving its strong direct rays. In winter, the Northern Hemisphere receives rays which are weaker and indirect because the Northern Hemisphere is tipped away from the sun. The sun is actually closer to the earth in winter and farther away in the summer. While marking your calendar, note that on June 30 half the year has gone by!

Activities

1. Read the Greek myth *Demeter and Persephone* which explains the reasons for seasons according to ancient Greek lore. Find other old tales and nature myths of different national origins that have quite different versions of how the seasons came to be. Which ancient group of people have the most exotic explanation?

2. The polar regions have only a dark and a light season. In the tropics there are no seasons, as we know them in the Northern Hemisphere, but only a variance of rainfall. Decide on a region of the world and create your own nature myth. Make up names of the central characters that fit the style of your myth. It's up to you! Don't be afraid of a humorous interpretation—your main characters could be Gorgonzola, Mozzarella, Monterey Jack, Roquefort or Port du Salut!

GA1153

3. The Four Seasons

Summer Fall Winter Spring

Summer Fall Winter Spring—
We remember everything!

Summer—hot
Fall—cool
Winter—cold
Spring—new!

Moving from the winter freezes
Into spring and summer breezes
Welcoming the falling leaves-es
And the bracing change of seasons!

Greta B. Lipson

7

GA1153

Lesson 4: Autumn

The September equinox is the beginning of autumn or the fall season. This is a particularly beautiful time of year with its warm days and cool evenings. It is also harvesttime. The night frosts begin to signal the onset of winter, and the birds start to migrate south as nature slowly prepares us with previews of winter storms. Late in the fall comes the glorious time of Indian summer when south winds bring in warm air northward over the country. The balmy, mild weather lasts for about two weeks before the onset of winter. The Indians believed that this brief, radiant time of year was a gift sent by the god of the Southwest.

In response to the question, "Why do the leaves fall?"—a growth of cells in the stem (petiole) of the leaf closes off the flow of water to the blade. The leaf cannot make food without water, and the green chlorophyll begins to disappear. For a few days the leaf dangles from a lifeless stem, and some newly formed colors begin to show themselves. The slightest wind encourages a fall of leaves. The leaves of most trees turn only one color in the fall, but the maple tree, with more varied color than any other, blazens into a rich fall tapestry.

Activities

1. Fall is synonymous with football. People are rarely indifferent to this exciting sport that commands millions of fans. But that doesn't mean that everybody enjoys the game. Here is a chance to express your opinion *in one succinct sentence.* In a "round robin" session, each person will begin by saying, "I like (dislike) football because. . . ." Here's your chance.

2. Describe football, from your point of view, from A to Z. Write a descriptive phrase or sentence moving through the alphabet. Underline the designated alphabet word. Start with the title "Alphabet Football."

   Example:

   A is for athletic ability.
   B is for battling your opponents.
   C is for crushing body offense.

   Mount the best of these efforts on tagboard, decorated with a border of leaf rubbings.

8

GA1153

4. Autumn

Fall Shadings

WHAT IS FALL?

A palette of burnished colors
Orange, brown, gold, crimson
Falling, twisted, curling, leaves
Winds blowing September memos
A patchwork of autumn tatters tossed helter skelter
Ombre splashes on a chestnut canvas
Remnants of sun-soaked glory
A sad bracing good-bye to summer.
Chilly promises of harsh winter

THAT IS FALL!

Greta B. Lipson

9

GA1153

Lesson 5: Banned Books Week

The purpose of this event is "to bring to the attention of the general public the importance of the freedom to read and the harm censorship causes to our society." It is sponsored by the American Library Association, American Booksellers Association, American Society of Journalists and Authors, the Association of American Publishers, National Association of College Stores, and American Association of University Presses.

Feelings run high in the debate on censorship because it is the practice of repressive governments to destroy books and prohibit free expression. Many well-intentioned people from all backgrounds and persuasions have protested books they considered unsuitable for young people. Some books which many authorities consider classics have been censored. It is a difficult problem to resolve since many people view censorship as a violation of the first amendment of our Constitution which guarantees Freedom of Speech, and the Press. Among the countless books that have been censored or removed from school libraries are

Goldings' *Lord of the Flies*

Dahl's *Charlie and the Chocolate Factory*

Anne Frank's *Diary of a Young Girl*

White's *Charlotte's Web*

The folktale *Little Black Sambo*

The Holy Bible

Mother Goose

Sendak's *In the Night Kitchen*

Huxley's *Brave New World*

American Heritage Dictionary

Shakespeare's *Macbeth*

Orwell's *1984*

In the book, *Now upon a Time*, by Myra P. Sadker, the author states, "Any book is a potential target of censorship. There are no totally safe, universally acceptable, uncontroversial books." (Harper & Row, Inc., © 1977, NY)

Activities

1. After a discussion of censorship, write two paragraphs. In one paragraph *defend* the censorship of books. Give reasons and a good defense for your point of view. In the second paragraph *oppose* censorship. Consider two points—*who* will censor, and *what* will they censor.

2. Study the poem on the opposite page which is called a diamante (Italian for diamond). Write your own diamond-shaped diamante which captures opposite concepts according to the directions on the following page.

GA1153

5. Banned Books Week

A Book Diamante

BOOK

**Informative, Powerful
Inspiring, Illuminating, Edifying
Treasures, Resources—Waste, Dross
Banned, Burned, Choked
Abyss, Darkness**

BLANK

Greta B. Lipson

Directions for a Diamante Poem:

Line 1: Topic noun (decide on an opposite ending noun)

Line 2: Two adjectives describing the topic

Line 3: Three action words (verbs or *ing* action words)

Line 4: Two words to describe topic noun and two words to describe the ending noun which is an antonym (opposite noun)

Line 5: Three action words for ending noun

Line 6: Two describing words for ending noun

Line 7: Ending noun, an antonym (opposite) of the topic noun

Lesson 6: Native American Indian Day

When the European explorers came to this country, they found Indians who had already been here for 20,000 to 40,000 years. It is assumed that Indians came from Asia, but this has not been established with certainty. Indians taught white settlers a vast number of survival skills. But in return the European settlers took over the lands of the Indians and ultimately forced them onto reservations. The conquest of Indians by the whites marked the decline of the Indian way of life everywhere in America. The census counts 1,400,000 Indians now living in the U.S. The quality of their lives is marked by extreme poverty, sub-standard housing, bad health, and unemployment. Indian illiteracy is among the highest in the nation. There are about 285 federal and state reservations, most located west of the Mississippi River. Indians and other concerned citizens have organized to redress some of the injustices imposed upon this proud people, over the centuries. Though forced to sacrifice land, wealth, customs and their civil rights, Indians were not granted U.S. citizenship until June 15, 1924. The purpose of Native American Indian Day is to honor and recognize the rich cultural heritage of Native Americans and their contribution to this country.

Activities

1. Given the significant contributions of the American Indians to the country, write a paragraph or a one-page paper persuading your legislator to create a National Native American Indian Day. List your reasons for your suggestion and be convincing.

2. Ask your school librarian to direct you to historical or current sources which deal with the problems experienced by Native Americans in their struggle for equality. Make notes of just one problem to present to the class. Write to the following organizations to learn about their activities: Association on American Indian Affairs, Inc., 95 Madison Ave., New York, NY 10016; United Indian Development Association, 9650 Flair Dr., #303, El Monte, CA 91731; The American Indian Movement, 1259 Folsom St., San Francisco, CA 94103.

GA1153

6. Native American Indian Day

Indian Voices

To understand a people and their history
It is they who must speak
About:
The erosion of the Indian heritage
Broken treaties
Their land taken away
Their nations destroyed
Tribes from Maine to Alaska
People of faith—their rights trampled.
The loss of customs—the corrosion of pride
Poverty on Indian reservations
Roads paved over sacred places
Northwestern forests violated
Mining—desecrating religious sites
Condos hunkering over burial grounds
Human remains
Both dead and alive.

Greta B. Lipson

GA1153

Lesson 7: Pickled Pepper Week

Pickled Pepper Week is not a great moment in history, but it is funny, it is good for a smile and it is a way to promote a product. In the world of business many companies capitalize on the charm, humor, beauty or ugliness of natural or manufactured products. The purpose of Pickled Pepper Week sponsored by Pickle Packers International, Inc., is to acquaint consumers with the zest provided by all the kinds of pickled peppers, such as bell, banana, cherry, chili, peperoncini, and all other sweet, hot, and mild peppers in the nightshade family that are stuffed into jars. The peppers which are grown in North and South America are the garden variety which are pickled for the palates of those who like a steamy or stimulating addition to their food. The yield of pepper plants is called fruit and may be green, yellow, or red. Peppers come in long or round shapes in varying sizes. The chemical which makes hot peppers hot is a compound called capsaicin, a part of the plant's defense. Interestingly, though capsaicin may cause a burning sensation on the hands of people who work with peppers or may burn the inside of your mouth, that hot chemical is benign once inside your digestive system! Studies have proven that hot peppers are kind to your stomach. So eat away to your stomach's delight. (Don't neglect International Pickle Week in May. It's all in the same family!)

Activities

1. Obviously, Peter Piper could not have picked his peppers already pickled but for the sake of alliteration we suspend our criticism. In the style of "Peter Piper" write your own alliteration about your favorite foodstuff. Give an award or a round of applause for the longest, alliteration.

   Percy Perkins picks perky peppers for his peppy pal, Patty, who packs pickled peppers in pints for her pappy who lives in Pittsfield where there's a paucity of peppers for poor people who are pepper fans!

2. Did you ever wonder about adventures in eating? The question of who was the first courageous soul to try certain foods begs to be answered. You may do some research about the real people who dared to try! Write a paragraph in which you create the event as you think it could have happened. Who was the first to eat:

   - lobster
   - pineapple
   - liver
   - tomato

GA1153

7. Pickled Pepper Week

Praise Pickled Peppers

Peter Piper picked a peck of pickled peppers
A peck of pickled peppers
Peter Piper picked.

He picked those pickled peppers
For Pickled Pepper Week
With a fervent pulsing passion for the fruit.
He wanted to pay homage
To the zest of pickled peppers
So he called the people packing
At the pickled pepper plant.

The workers sang the praises
Of the luscious pickled peppers
Crooning *a capella* phrases of a
    pickled pepper chant.

Here's a partial list of peppers:
Hot and mild, sweet and pungent
Dill, banana, bell and gherkin
Cherry, Polish, jalapeno
All prepared to please the public
From the pickled pepper plant!

Greta B. Lipson

15

Lesson 8: National Popcorn Poppin' Month

The consumption of that all-American treat popcorn started in North and South America with the Indians who raised popcorn before the Europeans arrived in the 1400's. The figures are staggering. Americans eat 383 million pounds of popcorn per year. Now that popcorn is made at home, 192 million pounds are prepared in American kitchens in all types of cookware. Each red-blooded American is calculated to consume two pounds per person annually. Popping corn is a special kind of corn—it has smaller, harder kernels than most field corn but has the same food value. The tough little kernels pop at a temperature of 400° F. When the internal moisture of the kernel heats to steam, the pressure explodes the kernel and *voila* there's the popcorn! A good quality kernel expands to about thirty times its original size when popped. Corn for popping is grown in Indiana, Iowa, Nebraska, and Ohio. Van Buren, Indiana, has declared itself the popcorn center of the world. They have the statistics to prove it and they have their very own popcorn festival.

Activities

1. Orville Redenbacher, who experimented with gourmet corn, was the first one to introduce quality popcorn to supermarkets. Redenbacher had a degree in agronomy and was determined to succeed. If you were to market your favorite food and introduce it to the public for the first time, what would the trade name of your snack be? How would you describe its flavor and appearance? Plan a logo for your product and write some tricky advertising copy that would really sell it. Even if your favorite food has been around for years, pretend no one but you knows about it.

2. There are times when you have had a luscious tub of popcorn in your lap and were watching a big thrilling event! Write a paragraph describing a movie or sports event that had you hypnotized while you ate your popcorn with machine-like intensity.

16

GA1153

8. National Popcorn Poppin' Month

It's Popping Its Little Heart Out

Do you want some?
No, I'm not hungry.
Are you sure?
I never change my mind!

Is something wrong?
What's that I hear?
What's it sound like?
Something's burping.
That's not burping—that's popcorn popping its little heart out!

What's that I smell?
What's it smell like?
Butter and heaven rolled into one!
That's popcorn popping its little heart out.

Do you want some?
Oh, do I ever!
You said you never change your mind.
I changed my mind.

How come?
You know the popcorn that's popping its little yellow heart out?
Yes.
It's popping its little heart out for me!

Greta B. Lipson

Lesson 9: Columbus Day

Columbus Day (originally called Discovery Day) falls on the second Monday of October. It is a holiday commemorating the discovery of America by Christopher Columbus in 1492. Columbus was a sailor and a navigator. He was Italian by birth (Christoforo Colombo 1451-1506) and became an explorer in the service of the Spanish government where Queen Isabella named him Admiral of the Ocean Sea. In Europe people were eager for the great riches in the East Indies—which at this time meant China, Japan and India. The trip to the Orient was a long, expensive overland route. The Portuguese were trying to find a sea route around Africa. But Columbus thought he could find a shorter sea route to the Indies. He did not expect to find a new world, nor was it his intention to prove the world round. It was his plan to sail due west to get east to the Asian shore, but he did not know that North and South America lay to the west between Europe and Asia. He left Spain with three ships, the *Nina*, the *Pinta*, and the *Santa Maria*. After seventy-two days Columbus and his ninety member crew arrived at San Salvador in the Bahamas, which he thought were islands of the Indies. He called them the West Indies, and he named the gentle people living there Indians. It was not known until after Columbus died that he had not reached the Indies but had reached the Western Hemisphere instead. In New York, on Columbus Day, there is a yearly parade of about 100,000 people among which Italian Americans participate in large and enthusiastic numbers!

Activities

1. If you could bring Christopher Columbus back to life, and you were a TV news anchorperson, what kinds of questions would you ask him about his life?

2. You, as an explorer astronaut, have been asked to speak to a group of taxpayers whose money and support you need badly. What would you say to convince them that space is a new frontier to explore for the benefit of civilization? What may there be to learn about in space? Or—perhaps you are a member of the audience who believes that our tax money is better spent by taking care of problems right here on Earth. Organize a pro and con discussion. Why do people explore, anyway?

18

GA1153

9. Columbus Day

Sail Columbus

The queen gave three ships
To Columbus one day.
He wanted to sail
To a land far away.

To look for a place
Full of riches and gold,
He went west to get east
To this land 'round the globe.

He wasn't quite sure—
Yes, we know that today
But isn't it great
That he went the wrong way?

Greta B. Lipson

Lesson 10: Migration of Birds

With the change of seasons, many birds migrate very long distances. In the fall they fly to a southern climate, since it is hard for them to find food in the ice and snow of the northern winter. In the spring they return once again. Birds make the trip at almost the same time each year and choose a particular route or flyway for the journey. There are four major flyways in North America. Birds have different styles of travel as well, since some travel in flocks and others fly alone. Some birds are nighttime travelers and others fly only by day. Many birds fly directly south, but others, less hurried, take a more indirect route. There are many mysteries in the matter of bird migration which have not been solved: Why do birds fly unerringly to their destination and never get lost? What makes them leave when they do each year? Why don't all birds of the same species leave at the same time? Why do many of them leave their northern homes before the weather gets cool? Scientists believe that birds are affected by changes in sunlight, which creates hormonal changes that give them the signal to travel to a different climate.

Activities

1. You are a newspaper reporter whose editor has sent you to Hinckley, Ohio, on March 15. Your assignment is to write about the "buzzard watchers" who travel to Hinckley to watch the buzzards fly back in the spring. The flock numbers from fifty to seventy-five birds. This return flight has been happening for 160 years, when the birds leave their winter home in the Smoky Mountains to return to rear their young in Ohio. The birds are also known as turkey vultures or carrion crows, and the people who come to watch may hang around all day waiting for the great return event! It's a great experience for all the townsfolk whose vigil is written about in every newspaper in the land.

2. Look in the *World Book Encyclopedia* for incredible answers to these questions:

   What bird is
   - the highest flyer (Bar-Headed Goose)
   - the fastest diver (Peregrine Falcon)
   - the largest bird (Male African Ostrich)
   - the smallest bird (Bee Hummingbird)
   - the greatest traveler (Arctic Tern)
   - the deepest diver (Common Loon of North America)

GA1153

10. Migration of Birds

Good-bye Songbirds

Who tells you
That it's time to go?
Who tells you
Of the coming snow?

Who tells you
To fly back in spring?
Who tells you
All is flowering?

Who tells you
Of my fresh delight
When I see songbirds
Back in flight?

Greta B. Lipson

GA1153

Lesson 11: Statue of Liberty Birthday

The full name of the Statue of Liberty is "Liberty Enlightening the World." It has been standing at the entrance to New York Harbor on Ellis and Liberty Islands since 1884. It is as arresting a sight today as it was when immigrants first arrived on American shores. The statue was sculpted by a Frenchman, Frédéric A. Bartholdi, who also selected the spot where Liberty would stand. The statue was given to Americans as an enduring gift of the French people. It was intended to honor our mutual regard for freedom under a democratic government. Liberty stands, in graceful flowing robes, holding the torch of liberty high in her right hand. On her left arm rests a tablet which has inscribed on it the date of the Declaration of Independence. On her head she wears a glorious crown with spikes which represent the rays of the sun and enlightenment. Down at her feet is found a broken shackle symbolizing the overthrow of tyranny and the rule of force. The copper statue is one of the largest ever made. It weighs 450,000 pounds and stands 151.1 feet tall. Visitors may take an elevator up the pedestal to the foot of the statue where there is an observation window. The more adventurous may climb a spiral staircase from the pedestal to the crown on Ms. Liberty's head. She will always be one of the most enthralling symbols of liberty any country has ever known!

Activities

1. In 1972 the American Museum of Immigration was built to memorialize the first wave of immigrants. The people in your family who came to this country as immigrants arrived at a port of entry or crossed a land border. Some of these entry points may have been Ellis Island in New York, San Francisco, Seattle, San Diego, Detroit or Brownsville, Texas. Do some family research. Ask your relatives to name the country they left and the U.S. city where they arrived. Be prepared to contribute to a class list, for example, Hong Kong to San Francisco; Canada to Detroit; Mexico to Laredo, Texas; Poland to New York; Vietnam to Los Angeles; Puerto Rico to Miami; Iraq to Detroit.

2. If you could emigrate to any city in the world today, which one would it be? What do you find attractive about the location you chose? What other information would you consider necessary to know before making the move? Why?

11. Statue of Liberty Birthday

The New Colossus

(Inscribed on a tablet in the pedestal of the Statue of Liberty in 1903)

Not like the brazen giant of Greek fame,
    With conquering limbs astride from land to land;
    Here at our sea-washed, sunset gates shall stand
A mighty woman with a torch, whose flame
Is the imprisoned lightning, and her name
    Mother of Exiles. From her beacon-hand
    Glows world-wide welcome; her mild eyes command
The air-bridged harbor that twin cities frame.
"Keep ancient lands, your storied pomp!" cries she
    With silent lips. "Give me your tired, your poor,
Your huddled masses yearning to breathe free,
    The wretched refuse of your teeming shore.
Send these, the homeless, tempest-tost to me,
    I lift my lamp beside the golden door!"

Emma Lazarus
1849-1887

Lesson 12: Halloween Witch

Halloween grew out of an ancient pagan festival which has survived throughout the years. According to ancient superstition, witches, goblins and assorted evil spirits came out on the eve of October 31 to worship the devil. Many of these creatures were supposed to be souls of the dead, revisiting the places they knew and wandering anywhere over the earth they chose to go. In England in anticipation of this yearly nocturnal visit, the people would dance around large bonfires making fearful noises to frighten away the witches and their kin. Witches were believed to have received powers from evil spirits. Witchcraft has been practiced for centuries in cultures all over the world. The word *witch* is derived from a word meaning "magician." Men who had these strange powers were called warlocks or sorcerers. Witches were able to ride on brooms, make themselves invisible, change into different creatures and (most important) cast spells over people and animals. American colonists brought their notions about witches and their craft to America, where the most notorious hunt took place in Salem, Massachusetts. In contemporary times, witches and Halloween have become the delightful property of the young. Along with it, we have trick or treating, a concept which has religious origins. In Ireland the *poor* would beg for *soul cake*. Those who contributed were blessed with good fortune while those who did not contribute were supposedly in for lots of trouble from spirits.

Activities

1. The witches in Shakespeare's *Macbeth* chanted, "Double, double, toil and trouble; Fire burn and cauldron bubble." Since then folklore has been rich with characters (good and bad) who cast charms, spells or blessings on others. Because you are good guys, work up some blessings, charms and spells that only do great things for people. For example:

   A Blessing: Watch over me from feet to ears
                 Protect me through the passing years.
   A Spell: May billows of rain clouds
                 Visit the school athletic field
                 And wash out the other team.

2. To the teacher: Have a spooky story hour. Play spooky music as the students enter the room. Turn out the lights and burn a single small lamp. Dress as a witch and read the spookiest, scariest stories you can find.

GA1153

12. Halloween Witch

Winnie the Witch

If you want to know the truth,
I'm too old for this stuff.
Climbing on uncomfortable broom handles,
Flying my poor old bones around in a dark sky,
With my clothes flapping in the wind.

My eyesight isn't as good as it once was,
In the dark.
And I never was good at directions.

Maybe I could cut the trip short
This October
And get home early with Felix, my cat.
(He's not getting any younger either.)
We could each have a cup of catnip tea,
With jack-o'-lantern muffins,
Enjoy a warming fire in the fireplace,
To coax the dampness out.
And talk about old times.

Nobody would know the difference.

Greta B. Lipson

GA1153

Lesson 13: Halloween Cat

The black cat is part of our Halloween lore because superstitious people believed that witches and evil spirits could turn themselves into cats at will. And everybody knows that a witch never made a trip on her broomstick without taking her cat along. Since early times fearful people have invested cats with supernatural and other worldly powers. Cats have an ancestry that goes back thousands of years. Indeed, they appear in ancient Egyptian art 4000 years ago. They were a decorative motif throughout that civilization. They were also revered as gods. This was demonstrated by the sun goddess Bubastis, who had the head of a cat. Egyptians who lost their cats would mourn them seriously by shaving their own eyebrows to demonstrate their grief. They would mummify their cats (and mice and rats to accompany them) and inter them in a pet cemetery. Cats were brought to America by the colonists in 1700. But cats have always had an aura of mystery and sinister legend surrounding them. Perhaps it is because they are so aloof— so elegant and self-contained, as if they have secrets they will not reveal. Their eyes, with their narrow pupils, appear to be ominous and all-knowing. But whether they bring good luck or bad luck they are permanent characters in Halloween lore!

Activities

1. Explain what the following cat sayings mean: "Curiosity killed the cat" (Mind your own business or you will get into trouble). "When the cat's away the mice will play." (If you're not being watched you may get reckless.) "Don't let the cat out of the bag." (Don't reveal the secret.) "Don't be catty." (Don't be a gossip.) "He's a cat's paw." (A person who is used by another as a tool to do something bad or distasteful.) Help brainstorm the longest list of "cat" adjectives ever seen!

2. Make a window cat. Cut out two black circles, one large and one smaller, to represent a cat's head and body. Add two pointed ears, skinny whiskers and a spiral tail that curls. To make a spiral tail, start with a large circle of paper 4½ inches in diameter. Start cutting from the outside, going around and around until the center is reached. Attach to the cat's back side. Paste cat on the classroom window, as if the cat is looking out and you are looking at his back.

GA1153

13. Halloween Cat

Cat Cries

Soft and furry
Black and purring
Crooning to the yellow moon

Catch the sparkle of cat eyes
Hear the screeching of cat cries
Piercing through the darkened skies
Living out nine promised lives.

Witches flying
Goblins crying—
Halloween will end too soon.

Greta B. Lipson

27

GA1153

Lesson 14: Halloween Owl

The owl takes its place among Halloween creatures for many reasons. Most owls are nocturnal, and their eerie hooting comes floating out of the forest at night, sounding like whoo, hoo-hoo, whoo. The owl's appearance is rather odd, and probably because of this, many legends connect him with witches, ghosts, calamity and death. Since the time of the Greeks, the owl has been associated with wisdom. He looks wise, but we are doubtlessly fooled by his solemn appearance. He has a large, broad head, with a ruff of feathers around his eyes. Unlike other birds, he looks straight ahead at the world with both bright yellow orbs. The owl's eyes are fixed in their sockets, and he cannot move them around. His head, however, is highly mobile, and he is able to turn it almost completely around in all directions. At night his pupils dilate so that he can hunt well in the dark. Other qualities make him a successful predator as well, for his feathers are so soft that his wings make no noise when he is in flight. Animals cannot hear him as he silently swoops down to the ground to snatch up mice and other rodents for his supper. Because of his eating habits, the owl is considered the farmers' friend, and in many states, he is protected by law. Depending upon its type, a full-grown owl may be two feet long or six inches long.

Activities

1. Describe the smartest person you know. Do you admire this person or not? Explain. Can people be smart in different ways? What does *street smart* mean?

2. A simile is a figure of speech that makes comparisons between two dissimilar things using the words *like, as, than . . . .* Just as the owl is used to represent a human trait, think of other creatures which are sometimes used to describe people. Use similes like sly as a fox, graceful as a gazelle, snappish as a crocodile, happy as a loon, slippery as an eel.

GA1153

14. Halloween Owl

Give a Hoot

Look! See the hoot owl—
All feathers and eyes.
He sees in the night,
For that's when he flies!

He's supposed to be smart,
Or that's what I'm told.
I have reason to doubt
That he's clever and bold.

Don't be impressed
By a smart-looking kisser,
He could be just as dumb
As your little sister!

To test his bird wisdom
Give him a word test.
If he knows which is witch
Then he's one of the best!

He'll be useful on All Hallow's Eve.

Greta B. Lipson

29

GA1153

Lesson 15: Halloween Mask

One of the fascinating staples of the Halloween masquerade has long been the wearing of grotesque, funny, or fashionable little masks that only cover the eyes and bridge of the nose. But masks didn't originate with Halloween. In ancient times people donned animal heads to promote good magic for hunting and life's events. Masks may also have been an offshoot of face markings which primitive peoples used to commune with the spirit world. As with many customs, the creation of masks is a rich expression of cultural folk art. Masks are used for ceremonies, as among the Indians. Theatrical masks were used by the ancient Greeks. The Chinese and the Japanese used masks in their classical dramas. Personalized burial and death masks were created by the ancient Egyptians. Contemporary revelers used festival masks for religious processions such as Mardi Gras in New Orleans. Throughout history the mask has been imbued with magical and spiritual powers; it transforms a face, it conceals and disguises, it hides the true person behind it and it can be most disquieting for the observer. Whatever your choice of mask, be it weird, simple, or gorgeous—be aware, on Halloween eve, that anything that obscures your vision to any degree can be a very real hazard!

Activities

1. A challenging and sophisticated Halloween art project starts with a simple supermarket paper bag. First fit it over your head to position it for your eyes and nose. If that does not serve your artistic plan, you may want to create the mask for display and not to wear. Use paint or magic marker or crayons in strong colors. Make the mask as dramatic and bold as you can on a large scale. Don't rush the project; this could take days. Accessorize your bag with anything that will make it look spectacular, such as sequins, feathers, straw, or strips of cloth! Line the masks up, side by side, to see how wild and fanciful they are. Invite other classes in. Have a judging by students from other rooms. Display them!

2. If you were to hide behind the face of a famous person, who would it be? Why?

15. Halloween Mask

Fright Mask

I can't explain
The fright I feel.
All gruesome masks
To me seem real!

The twisted mouth
The wicked eyes
The pointy teeth—
A bad surprise.

And really,
Though I know it's you
(My closest friend
I know from school)

I'm still a wreck
When you say, "BOO!"

Greta B. Lipson

31

GA1153

Lesson 16: Invention of the Sandwich

In America's melting pot there are tasty treats of every description contributed by every ethnic group that has come to this country. We are enormously enriched by these recipes, and we are fattened up by the cuisine that has found its way into grateful American stomachs. Of all the people who have contributed to our menu, we owe, perhaps, the greatest debt to an English nobleman of the 1700's—John Montagu, the 4th Earl of Sandwich. The mention of his name inspires instant recognition for it was he who was the inventor of the sandwich in 1762. The story of his discovery places him at a gaming table which he refused to leave for twenty-four hours. He was an inveterate gambler known for his staying power and his wealth! Though reluctant to leave the card game, he felt a consuming hunger descend upon him for which he found a quick solution. He ordered a servant to bring him a piece of roast beef between two pieces of bread and behold—the sandwich was born! The quick snack caught on and became part of the fashionable cuisine of Europe. The word *sandwich* was introduced into the French language shortly thereafter.

Activities

1. For a fun time find the poem "Peanut-Butter Sandwich" by Shel Silverstein in his collection *Where the Sidewalk Ends*. It is a poem about a dippy young king whose passion for p.b. sandwiches nearly destroys him! For an even bigger treat, locate a tape of Shel Silverstein reciting that very same poem. (Harper & Row, Inc., 53rd St., NY 10022)

2. An *eponym* is a word that is derived from a person's name. Some of those words are very familiar to us though we may not know the history of the person responsible. Some examples are Jules Leotard, a French circus acrobat; the Frisbee baking family (think aluminum pie plate); and Levi Straus an immigrant who sold canvas pants to miners in California. Now it's your turn to name an exciting product after yourself that will go down in history. Include a history of the fascinating way the product came into existence! If you need help, you may borrow a product that is already in existence, and pretend you invented it! _____ tape, _____ tissues, _____ duplicating machine. For more clues, read the book *Take My Word for It* by Vernon Pizer, Dodd & Mead Co., New York, 1981.

 GA1153

16. Invention of the Sandwich

Happy Birthday, Earl of Sandwich
(1718-1792)

Bless your heart, Earl of Sandwich.
Without you we wouldn't have a hamwich.

What would we do
With our peanut butter and jelly,
How on earth would it get into our belly?

Where would we put
Our tasty fresh lunch meat?
It would turn slime green and wouldn't be a lunch treat!

How would we make
A toasted B.L.T.,
Without creating a calamity?

Thank heaven, Earl of Sandwich,
That you were so smart,

And once again we bless
Your inventive dear heart!

Greta B. Lipson

33

Lesson 17: Basketball Founder's Birthday

Basketball was invented in the U.S. in 1891 by a physical education teacher, James Naismith, who was employed at the Y.M.C.A. Training School in Springfield, Massachusetts. Naismith's department head asked him to create a game that could be played indoors or out. Naismith worked out a team sport with eighteen men on a team since that was the number of students enrolled in the class. In order to play the game he needed two baskets suspended from the balcony of the gym. When the janitor attached two half-bushel baskets (used for peaches), they worked so well that his innovation became the basis for the name of the sport. Everything about the sport was so fascinating to sports enthusiasts that news of it circulated wildly throughout the U.S. and Canada. Basketball has evolved in the past 100 years but is still flexible enough to be played solo, by teams or with just a couple of participants. The most significant change in the game affected the basket. In the early stages of basketball every time a player made a basket the ball would get stuck in the basket and would have to be freed by someone on a ladder. The backboard of the basket was added to eliminate audience interference and the rim of the basket was changed to metal. It is hard to believe that this sport—dreamed up by a teacher in response to his boss's request—would grow to become the most highly attended sport in the country. Basketball's fans are numbered literally in the millions. It is played in schools, colleges, professional arenas, side drives and in back alleys and in every place a basket can be attached to a support.

Activities

1. Decribe a basketball game or other game you attended where the plays drove the crowd wild with enthusiasm. What occurred at the game? This is an opportunity to bring into class an exciting account of a great game from the sports section of your newspaper.

2. For rare sports poetry read "The Base Stealer" by Robert Francis and "Foul Shot" by Edwin A. Hoey in the collection *Reflections on a Gift of Watermelon Pickle*, edited by Stephen Dunning, et al, Lothrop, Lee & Shepard Co., 1967. Search for more sports poetry. It does exist!

GA1153

17. Basketball Founder's Birthday

I Dream Myself Tall

Myself, I'm short
But when I see those two teams
Run onto the court
And see those ten tall people—
I DREAM MYSELF TALL!

That's me.
Right in the middle of the action
Starting with that center jump
Touching the ball and tapping it
To my teammates.

In the fast break
We're on the offensive
I'm like lightning
Moving swiftly for the pass.
My wrists have that silky shooting touch.

I zip down court in a frenzy
Worm my way through the air
To sink an alley-oop!
The crowd roars.

Oh boy! Player's joy!
I'm the hottest shooter on the team.
I DREAM MYSELF TALL!

Greta B. Lipson

35

GA1153

Lesson 18: Thanksgiving Guests

The Pilgrims came to Massachusetts from England in 1620 and set up the colony of Plymouth on Cape Cod Bay. In their homeland the Pilgrims were forced to belong to the Church of England. Rather than endure persecution they left England in search of religious freedom. Their first winter in the New World was rigorous and cruel. At least half of the 101 passengers from the *Mayflower* did not survive. They were assisted out of their hardship by the Algonquin Chief Squanto and his tribe members who taught the Pilgrims to plant corn, fertilize their crops, hunt, fish and select edible wild plants for survival. Without this act of goodness the Massachusetts Bay colony would never have survived. The Pilgrims' second harvest reflected their new skills and life was kinder to them. By the decree of Governor William Bradford, they held a festival of Thanksgiving in 1621. Approximately eighty friendly Indians were invited to participate in this first joyous celebration where there was feasting, praying and singing. For many years to follow, the celebration of this harvest holiday was random and regional. Many different dates were observed throughout the country until Mrs. Sarah J. Hale, a journalist for the magazine *Godey's Lady's Book* rigorously promoted the idea of one set day of observance. In 1863 she wrote: ". . .would it not be more noble, more truly American, to become national in unity. . .in our tribute of joy and gratitude for blessings." President Lincoln responded favorably to her suggestion and was the first to establish a national day. This was later changed in 1941 by President Roosevelt to its present date which was deemed better for the economy. Thanksgiving Day is the unofficial start of the Christmas shopping season, and the day for the Macy's Thanksgiving Day Parade—the largest and most exciting in the country.

Activities

1. Under the classification of things we never think about, consider reading and reporting on the book by Ann McGovern, *If You Sailed on the Mayflower*. First answer these questions as a class, then find the author's answer. What kind of ship was the *Mayflower*? How many people sailed on it? Were the people on the ship friends? Did the kids get into trouble? Did the sailors like the Pilgrims? Where did the passengers eat, drink and sleep? What did they do about keeping themselves and their clothes clean? Did people get seasick? Did anybody die on board?

2. With a partner, work out your favorite Thanksgiving menu in detail. Look at the supermarket ads in the newspaper and calculate an approximate cost of your party. Decide on how many guests you will invite and plan to purchase in appropriate amounts. On your family invitation list, first write the names of family members and friends and then give them Indian names such as Running Mouth, Skinny Arrow, Lumbering Bear, Great Strong Arm, Whispering Butterfly.

GA1153

18. Thanksgiving Guests

R.S.V.P. Pilgrims and Indians

Do you like the taste of turkey?
Do you like to eat a lot?
Do you walk around the kitchen
And peek in all the pots?

Are you thankful for your blessings?
Do you smell the pumpkin pie?
Would Pilgrims and Indians like to stop by?

Greta B. Lipson

37

GA1153

Lesson 19: Thanksgiving Menu

It is difficult for modern people to realize the monotony of the meals eaten by the early settlers. Refrigeration was nonexistent and meals were made up largely of fruits and vegetables that would not rot in root cellars. When the Pilgrims had a Thanksgiving feast in 1621 it was probably the heartiest, most delicious meal they would have until the following spring. Wild turkey was, as we know, only one item on the menu. (These had first been domesticated by the Aztec and Zuñi Indians and were native to America.) There were also venison (deer meat), rabbit, fish, clams, succotash, nuts, fruits, journey cake, pies, cookies and more! A rundown of the menu would hardly be complete without a salute to Quadequina, the chief's brother, who brought the all-time American favorite! He took some corn seeds out of his deerskin bag and threw them on the hot rocks circling the cook fire. The rest is history! The Anglos from England ate their first popcorn. Everyone participated in the preparations for the feast. The mothers cooked for days and the children helped roast and turn the foods over open fires out-of-doors. Long wooden tables were set up under the trees so that everyone could spread out and enjoy the memorable three-day feast. (An historical footnote suggests that goose, not turkey, was their bird of choice.) Before eating the goose, the Pilgrims' custom was to tie the poor foul's feet together and toss him down the chimney so that his flapping wings would clean the soot and grime from the walls of the flue on his way down. The goose was an all-purpose creature whose feathers were used to stuff blankets and pillows, and his quills were used to make ink pens!

Activities

1. Everybody—young and old—needs a verbal thank-you, a pat on the back, or the admiration of others. Thanksgiving is the perfect time to express your appreciation to someone in your life who has been kind to you. As your personalized Thanksgiving gift, write a thank-you note to someone. Remember family, friends, school personnel, and others.

2. With the help of your school librarian, locate a colonial cookbook for fascinating information on utensils, recipes, and food preparation of the times. Example: *Slumps, Grunts & Snickerdoodles: What Colonial America Ate & Why*, by Lila Perl © 1975 Houghton Mifflin. Share information and make a presentation on one aspect of colonial food preparation you find especially interesting. Snickerdoodles are sugar cookies.

19. Thanksgiving Menu

Thanksgiving Is Delicious

From the moment
I walk
Through the door
The smells float
In welcome fragrance
Announcing to my
Nose and brain and appetite
The coming of the feast.

Empty belly
Ready to be filled
With
Succulent turkey
Rib-sticking stuffing
Billowy mashed potatoes
Slow moving gravy (tumbling with mushrooms)
Ruby red cranberry sauce
Woodsy green snap beans.

And don't forget dessert!
Ahh, golden pumpkin pie
Perky dollops of whipped cream
Apple dazzle tarts
With hidden currants winking.

Now slow to stop!
I cannot stuff any more into my body.
Let's rest a bit.
We'll see what happens later.

Greta B. Lipson

GA1153

Lesson 20: Hanukkah

Hanukkah, The Festival of the Lights, celebrates a victorious battle for religious freedom in ancient times. The holiday usually occurs in December and is celebrated by the Jews on the twenty-fifth day of the Hebrew month of Kislev. Hanukkah lasts for eight days and has its origins in the occurrence of a miracle over 2000 years ago in Palestine. Before the birth of Christ, a tyrant named Antiochus wanted the Jews to give up their holy books, to forsake the one God and to worship idols. A group of Jewish men called the Maccabees fought Antiochus IV for seven years, and finally drove his soldiers from Jerusalem. The Jews rejoiced and returned to rededicate their Temple and rekindle the eternal light in the Temple lamp. But they could find only one small jar of holy oil, which meant that the light would burn for only one night. They lit the menorah (candelabra) and a strange thing happened. The menorah continued to burn for eight long days, and all through that time the people held services dedicated to their victory over tyranny and the blessings of religious freedom. In acknowledgement of the miracle of the lights, Judas Maccabaeus, the Jewish leader, proclaimed a festival during which time the holiday spirit would prevail. Today, Jewish children re-enact the miracle of lights by lighting one candle each night for eight nights. In the middle of the menorah there is a ninth candle called the shammes. The shammes is lighted first and is used to light the other candles each night. The number of candles lit represents the day of the holiday (third day, three candles; fourth day, four candles). After the lighting of the menorah, the party begins with friends and family present. There is gift giving, singing, celebrating and loads of potato pancakes for everyone to eat. The children are given little spinning tops called dreidles, and on these are the Hebrew letters *NGHS*, which signify, "A great miracle happened here." The word *Hanukkah* means "dedication."

Activities

1. If the Jewish people in 165 B.C. had lost their battle for religious freedom and the right to worship one God, what possible implications would this have had for Christianity?

2. Here is a Hanukkah recipe that can be made at school or at home.

Hanukkah Potato Latkes (Pancakes)

Grate 4 large potatoes and 1 small onion

Add salt and pepper, 1 tablespoon pancake flour or all-purpose flour, 1 egg, pinch of baking powder (optional)

Mix together well. Heat oil or shortening in skillet. Use a soup tablespoon to spoon the batter into the skillet. This makes a nice modestly sized pancake. Fry on medium heat until golden brown. Drain the pancakes on paper toweling as you take them out of the pan. Eat with sour cream or applesauce. Enjoy!

Note to the cook: These latkes are very easy to make! The recipe need not be precise. This is a down-home recipe that is not sensitive or temperamental. It never fails, so be intrepid!

GA1153

20. Hanukkah

The Festival of Lights

(2000 years ago—165 years before the birth of Christ)

The tyrant, Antiochus IV swept into the temple of the Jews
With his military might.
"You must forsake your holy books
And your one God!" he thundered,
"Or face destruction."
But the Jews would not renounce their God!

Judas Maccabaeus, the Jewish leader, led the fierce revolt
As the people in Judea fought the tyrant who ravaged their temple.
Determined to win their precious rights of religious freedom,
They would not renounce their God!

The tyrant and his hordes
Fell back in ragged defeat
And were driven from Jerusalem.
At once, the triumphant Jews swept away the idols
Prepared to rededicate their house of worship.

With only one night's measure of oil
They rekindled the eternal light.
Strangely, the light at the altar
Burned for eight long days and nights—
In mysterious testimony to the sacred struggle
Of a people
Who would not renounce their God!

And God was given thanks
For victory over oppression
And the exalted gift of religious freedom!

Greta B. Lipson

41

GA1153

Lesson 21: Winter Holiday

The commercialism of holidays is of genuine concern to many people. The fear is that the excesses of gift-giving undermine the true meaning and spiritual value of the traditions we observe. A price tag attached to an object is evidence that can be calculated. More important gifts of the spirit have incalculable worth. It is not easy to make a commitment of friendship or affection and be called upon to demonstrate that commitment under demanding circumstances. To come through, to stand by, to be truly giving of your time, your patience, your support or understanding are the real gifts. We should be taught that the true meaning of giving is to offer that which is a portion of ourselves. One may strike a contrast between material gifts and the gift of love, which cannot be bought but is the most enduring of all human offerings.

Activities

1. Bring in any kind of box from home. Enclose the poem "The Most Precious Gift" in the box. Wrap the box or draw designs on it so that it can be offered as a unique gift of love for Hanukkah, Christmas, Kwanzaa or any special time when it would be welcome!

2. What are the important things we can give to others that do not have price tags? Discuss and list these on the chalkboard. Why do some people have a problem expressing or communicating kind and positive thoughts to friends and family? What are some of the things we can say to people that would make them feel good?

   - You did a great job!
   - Could you use some help?
   - You make other people feel good.
   - It was fun to be with you.
   - You are a comfortable kind of friend.
   - You always listen and understand.
   - You are special!

42

GA1153

21. Winter Holiday

The Most Precious Gift

The most precious gift,
I am told,
Is all the love
The heart can hold.

I give it to you;
You give it to me—
There's enough for the world,
And the gift is free.

Will you take my love—
More precious than gold?
It's the finest gift
That the heart can hold.

Greta B. Lipson

GA1153

Lesson 22: Christmas Santa

St. Nicholas was a real person! When he was still a boy, he was made the Bishop of Myra in an ancient city in Turkey in the fourth century A.D. He had a reputation for great kindness because during his lifetime he gave generously to the needy. He became known throughout Europe for his goodness. After his death he was made the patron saint of school children who celebrated a feast day in his name on December 6. It was the Dutch settlers who brought the tradition of Sinter Klaas to America in the 1600's. Children in this country said his name so rapidly that it ran together and assumed the sound of Santa Claus. (Try it!) When Santa first arrived he was, believe it or not, a tall, thin, distinguished looking person who wore a long red robe and rode an elegant horse. But a physical transformation occurred because of different interpretations in American literature and art. In 1809 the author Washington Irving described Santa as the guardian of New York in *Knickerbocker's History of New York*. Irving placed him in a wagon throwing presents down chimneys while riding over the treetops. Then along came Clement C. Moore in 1822 with his irresistible description of Santa in his poem "A Visit from St. Nicholas." It was Moore who gave him a big belly that shook like jelly and a fat, jolly appearance. The next rendition of Santa, which permanently fixed him in the minds and hearts of American children, was a painting by Robert Weir and a cartoon in the late 1800's by Thomas Nast. Gone forever was the elegant old guy of the Dutch settlers. Yet, however he has changed, Santa remains the embodiment of happiness and good cheer in the holiday season.

Activities

1. Put yourself in Santa's place. He has to travel miles and miles in one night. Make things easier for him by writing very detailed directions to your house. Include a carefully drawn map with north, south, east and west directions. Include any important landmarks in your community that will help him find his way. Check out the accuracy and "findability" of your directions with a partner in class. Discuss some of the important aspects of cartography (mapmaking) with the class. Don't be afraid to use humor!

2. Santa Claus, Indiana, is a real town that is 10 miles north of the Ohio River, and 30 miles northeast of Evansville, Indiana. (Find it on a map.) If you were to receive a letter from the town, it would have a postmark that reads, Santa Claus, IN. If you were interested, what might you personally do with that information? (Have a letter sent to a little sibling from Santa Claus, Indiana.)

GA1153

22. Christmas Santa

In Defense of Santa

Alert all cynics
On this day
Who would explain
Old Claus away
And ruin the joy
Of the holiday season
For various, sundry and
    miserable reasons!

There is a serious
Issue here
That we would like
To make perfectly clear.

It wouldn't do grown-ups
Any harm
To succumb to Santa's
    irresistible charm
And welcome his gift
Of yuletide pleasure
And yield to the fantasy
In full measure.
So, adults, keep childhood dreams
Intact
Or else you endanger your own—
In fact!

Greta B. Lipson

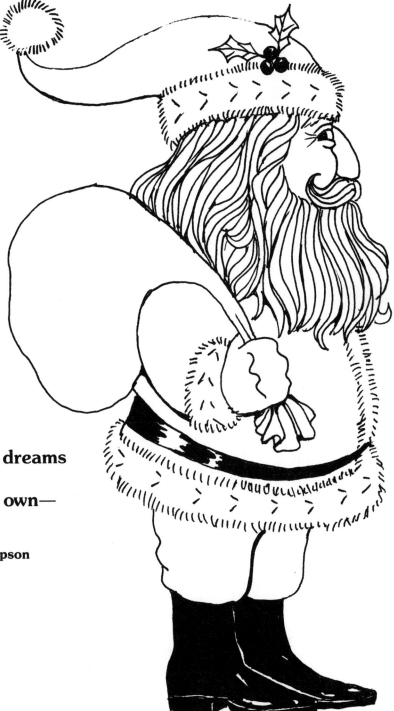

45

Lesson 23: Christmas Angel

An angel is a supernatural being sent by the Almighty to carry a divine message to all people. The conventional image of an angel is that of a human being with wings and a halo dressed in white robes and having an aura of goodness, innocence and beauty. Being possessed of greater than human intelligence and power, an angel may be the guardian of people and nations alike. The New Testament Bible tells us that on Christmas Eve the shepherds were out in the fields watching over their flocks at night when an angel appeared to bring them the joyous news of the birth in the manger. The sky over the fields was suddenly filled with angels and when they went away, the shepherds said, "Let us go over to Bethlehem and see this thing that has happened." Whether one's disposition is religious or nonreligious, the word *angel* is used and understood as a popular metaphor to mean a kind and giving person who may also be one's guiding light or influence in life.

Activities

1. Organize a drive for canned food for the needy. Make posters entitled, "Be an Angel—Give All You Can!" Make flyers with the same message to be sent home. Use an opaque projector and duplicate the Christmas Angel on the following page (see illustration) to be adapted for the hall posters.

2. Plan a class yuletide trip to a senior citizen facility or a children's ward in your local hospital. Prepare a program of holiday songs and music. Plan a visit to a community soup kitchen where class members can volunteer services for a designated number of hours. Make arrangements in advance with a social work agency where they can help coordinate class participation. You will brighten the lives of many people who will enjoy your youthful vitality, your wonderful faces, and your heartfelt gesture of holiday cheer. Be it known that the Recording Angel will remember your deeds!

46

GA1153

23. Christmas Angel

Christmas Angel

Christmas Angel sweet and dear,
Fills my heart with Christmas cheer.

Gifts of love, she too will pray,
Come to all on Christmas Day.

Greta B. Lipson

GA1153

Lesson 24: Christmas Tree

One of the legends of the use of the evergreen as a ceremonial tree begins in Germany over 1200 years ago when an English missionary, Winfrid (St. Boniface) had an encounter with Druid priests. They worshipped the oak tree and used it in the forest as a place for human sacrifice. When Winfrid cut down their oak tree, a young evergreen instantly grew back in its place. He convinced the Druids that the evergreen was to be their new holy tree of peace and Christ. The Germans were thought to have been the first people to decorate Christmas trees following the example of Martin Luther who had used symbolic candles as ornaments. Many nationalities use materials indigenous to their environment (the Scandinavians used little fishnets). The ancient custom of using evergreens to decorate homes and churches was brought to America by the Pilgrims who used—of course—strings of popcorn, cranberries, and homemade candy canes! The most notable Christmas tree in our time is the giant tree at Rockefeller Center at 1230 Avenue of the Americas, in New York City. This seventy-five-foot Norway Spruce is set aglow in a tree lighting ceremony every December 5, to herald the opening of the holiday season.

Activities

1. Make your own collage Christmas tree to demonstrate the imaginative possibilities of homemade holiday decorations. Outline your tree on a piece of cardboard. Collect every interesting item or bauble you can find, including ribbon, glitter, macaroni, buttons, yarn, wrapping paper, old greeting cards, patches of material. Make a flat collage Christmas tree with a wild variety of textures, shapes and colors. Display the startling results! The size is up to you. The first try may encourage you to go larger.

2. Imagine that you are an evergreen waiting to be chosen and sold to a family. Express in a paragraph the feelings you have when you are carried to the family's home. How does it feel to be decorated with glittering finery and fussed over endlessly? What happens when the holiday is over and you are stripped of your baubles, dried out and discarded? Make a mime presentation of the complete episode with several others. Ask for a volunteer narrator to enhance the drama. Is there a guitarist in the crowd to heighten the mood and action?

24. Christmas Tree

Evergreen

Who will trim thee,
Little tree—
Sharp and green
For all to see?
I will trim thee,
Little tree.
All the shining world
Will see
All your splendor,
Little tree.

Greta B. Lipson

49

GA1153

Lesson 25: Kwanzaa

Kwanzaa is an Afro-American holiday which was founded in 1966 by Maulana Ron Karenga. This celebration is a recognition of traditional African harvest festivals. *Kwanzaa* is a word in the Swahili language which means "first fruit." Though it is a new holiday in America, the custom of giving thanks for the bounty of nature is an ancient practice. The idea of this festival is to overcome the commercialization of the holiday season. Participants desire a holiday that celebrates the unity of the black family, the goal of community cooperation, and the nurturance of enduring cultural values. The celebration lasts seven days beginning with the lighting of a single candle in a kanara (candle holder). Each day a candle is lit as the theme of that day is discussed. Personal reflection and appreciation are emphasized. The festival themes are

*● December 26 umoja (unity)
● December 27 Kujichagulia (self-determination)
● December 28 ujima (group effort)
● December 29 ujamaa (group economics)
● December 30 Kuumba (creativity)
● December 31 nia (purpose)
● January 1 imani (faith)

The festivities come to a close on the final day when there is an exchange of small gifts called "zawadi." These gifts have been made with an investment of time and affection by family members for each other. Everyone then sits down to enjoy the final feast of Kwanzaa called a "karamu" at which time thanks are given for a plentiful harvest, for the profound good fortune of family and friends, and for the blessings of a peaceful and productive community.

Activities

1. Obviously the themes of Kwanzaa are significant to all people. Select, from the list above, three themes that are especially important to you. Explain why. How would you define each to the class?

2. If you had to give a gift to someone that you made yourself, what would it be? Assume that your funds are limited and you want the gift to be modest, special and meaningful. Are there many gift suggestions you can think of that would fit that description? What are they?

---

*Randy Harelson, *The Kids' Diary of Amazing Days* (New York: Workman Publishing, 1979).

25. Kwanzaa

African December

(*Kwanzaa* means "first fruit" in Swahili)

Make way for Kwanzaa,
It holds a radiant place
In African December.

Rejoice in the richness of the harvest
In the fragrance of African fruit—
Aromatic yield of the earth,
Bountiful, plentiful,
Overflowing in God's generosity.

In reverence for nature's abundance
Communal voices ring uplifted
In a harmony of prideful endeavor
Grateful for the gifts of human goodness
And the everlasting nurture of family ties.

Greta B. Lipson

GA1153

Lesson 26: National Whiner's Day

The intent of Kevin C. Zaborney, the founder of Whiner's Day, was to establish the very day after Christmas as a time of national observance when all the ingrates in the land could complain about the rotten and uninspired gifts they received for Christmas. That certainly seems to be an appropriate time to mark the calendar for whiners. We realize, however, that whining is an event that takes place, for some people, twelve months of the year. It is definitely not limited to December 26! The whining style deserves some time and analysis since it is unique and unmistakable. Most people recognize the whine and the irksome sound which causes the listener's cardinal humors and brain to swell with exasperation. The delivery is never hurried. It is slow, interminable and is distinguished by its nasality and rhythm. As the whine resonates through the nose, the sound is almost beyond human endurance. The refrain of the whine may vary from time to time. Some of the classic themes may be: "That's not fair." "But you promised." "Nobody told me." "You never listen to what I want." Changing the behavior of inveterate whiners is a challenging task. There is no known cure. Whiners have been known to marry one another; this seems to be a suitable solution.

Activities

1. On the chalkboard list all the whining complaints you have ever heard. Which are the most frequently heard in your class? Which ones do you hear the most at home? When your list is complete, ask for volunteers to read their choices of some especially good ones. Have a whiner's contest. Organize some role play episodes with a whiner and his/her victim.

2. Write an account of what you whine about the most. Justify your behavior with a convincing written argument. Discuss this affliction.

GA1155

26. National Whiner's Day

Wisdom for a Whiner

Don't be a wienie, Whining Willy
When you're wailing you're so silly
With your sniveling and complaining
All the time!

You're a hateful sort of person
We can tell, we're so discerning,
That there's no one in the world
Who treats you well.

Just ask yourself the question.
If you really truly care,
Why you think your life
Is never ever fair.

Stop whining through your nose and then
We'll all begin supposing
What would happen if you stopped
Your sad refrain.

Try smiling, Whining Willy
And be willing to stop whining
And we all will love you better
Day by day!

Greta B. Lipson

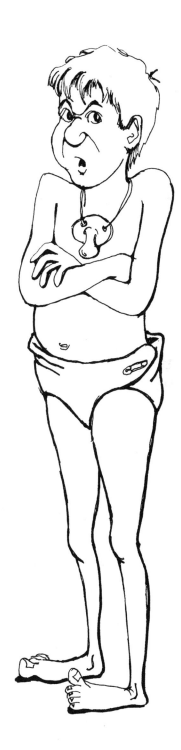

53

GA1153

Lesson 27: New Year's Day

Symbolism means the use of one thing to suggest something else—specifically the use of symbols to represent abstract ideas in concrete ways.

The New Year, and all its visual images, is replete with symbolism. In this case, the familiar old man represents the old year that is departing and the baby is the personification of the new year. We are happy to see a new year arrive since it gives us the fresh opportunity to make new resolutions.

January is named after the Roman god, Janus, who was the god of gates and doors (more symbolism). Because he was responsible for beginnings, Janus had two faces—one which looked back to what had passed and the other which looked forward into the future (quite a trick). It has been argued that January 1 is a strange day for the new year since it is not a marker for the sun's cycle. But since the introduction of the Gregorian calendar in 1582, Europeans and Americans have observed the January date in which to herald the New Year. This is a time to settle quarrels, reaffirm family ties and personally turn over a new leaf. Because January is the coldest month even the birds, animals and growing things are very quiet. It is a good time for insightful contemplation.

Activities

1. Discuss the meaning of a New Year's resolution in class. Make a New Year's resolution of your own. Perhaps you want to change or improve yourself in some way. Write out a contract just for you that says: On this New Year, January 19____, I hereby resolve to _____.
   Now sign your name to this document. Make it look official!

2. Take an inventory of yourself. First, make a list of things you really like about yourself. Use the heading "Good Qualities." Now make another list of things about yourself you know are not great with the heading "I'll Work on This!"

54

GA1153

27. New Year's Day

New Year's Resolution

This is the time that
I want to resolve
And announce to the world
That I want to solve
Some of the rotten things I do
And I am told
There are more than a few.

I want to behave in a way that's
Desirable
And make myself much more
Admire-able!

But if I falter,
I won't be discouraged,
I'll remember these words
And be encouraged:

Personal victory
Is a fine award.
Satisfaction, it's true,
Is the real reward!

So make that knockout resolution
And find a truly simple solution.
When you finally correct your behavior that's flawed,
The whole world will be incredibly awed.

Greta B. Lipson

55

GA1153

Lesson 28: Martin Luther King, Jr.'s, Birthday (1929-1968)

Martin Luther King, Jr., who was born in Atlanta, Georgia, was the son and the grandson of Baptist ministers. Dr. King was ordained a minister in 1947 when he was only eighteen years old. Reverend King lived in Montgomery, Alabama, with his wife, Coretta, and his children when he became the pastor of the Dexter Avenue Baptist Church in 1954. King was one of the greatest civil rights leaders in America during the 1950's and 1960's. He believed in nonviolent resistance in order to win civil rights for all people. In 1964 he was awarded the esteemed Nobel peace prize for his peaceful leadership of black people in their struggle for equality. In 1955 Dr. King received national attention as a civil rights leader when he led a boycott of buses in Montgomery, Alabama. At that time all black people in the South were obliged to sit in the back of the bus. Only whites were permitted to use the front of the bus. This particular issue was highly symbolic of the unequal treatment of Blacks throughout the United States. The success of this nonviolent campaign led to other peaceful demonstrations from 1955 to 1965. On August 28, 1963, more than 200,000 of King's supporters marched from the Washington Monument to the Lincoln Memorial in Washington, D.C. It was on that occasion that he made the most famous of his speeches. Congress enacted the Civil Rights Act of 1964 and the Voting Rights Act of 1965, which was in large part due to the efforts of this remarkable black leader. Martin Luther King, Jr., was shot in Memphis, Tennessee, on April 4, 1968, by James Earl Ray, an escaped convict who was sentenced to ninety-nine years in prison for this violent crime. President Lyndon B. Johnson declared a national day of mourning to honor Dr. King who was loved and admired by people of all races and creeds throughout the world. His birthday became a civil holiday by an act of Congress in 1983.

Activities

1. "We Shall Overcome!" Discuss the use of slogans at meetings, conventions and in the media. What is their function? (Answer: Slogans unify—they express a cause and its creed publicly, they provide a rallying point.) Express something in a slogan that is important to you and to other people, such as a school slogan. A slogan must have the impact of a headline that everyone understands immediately. Read some of your classmates' slogans and decide which are most effective. What makes them effective?

2. To understand the power of the spoken word, one must listen. Locate a recording of Martin Luther King delivering his famous speech, "I have a dream. . . ." Perhaps your school media teacher can locate other great speeches by Winston Churchill, President Roosevelt or other accomplished orators. You needn't listen from beginning to end to capture the speaker's intensity.

56

28. Martin Luther King, Jr.'s, Birthday

Salute to Martin Luther King, Jr.!

His dream inspired the lives
Of black and white people.

He led the poor,
Supported the weak,
Championed their cause.

He marched for his brothers and sisters
And fell—A Hero.

Greta B. Lipson

So I say to you, my friends, that even though we must face the difficulties of today and tomorrow, I still have a dream. It is a dream deeply rooted in the American dream that one day, this nation will rise up and live out the true meaning of its creed—"We hold these truths to be self-evident, that all men are created equal."

I have a dream that one day on the red hills of Georgia, sons of former slaves and sons of former slave owners will be able to sit down together at the table of brotherhood.

And when we allow freedom to ring. . .we will be able to speed up that day when all of God's children—black men and white men, Jews and Gentiles, Catholics and Protestants—will be able to join hands and sing in the words of the old Negro spiritual, "Free at last, free at last; Thank God Almighty, we are free at last."

Martin Luther King, Jr.

GA1153

Lesson 29: Chinese New Year

The Chinese lunar calendar dates back to the twenty-seventh century before Christ. According to that ancient calendar, the new year is set sometime between January 20 and February 20 at the time of the new moon. (The Gregorian calendar was adopted in China in 1912.) The Chinese calendar was 354 days—12 lunar months (half with 30 days and half with 29 days). Every two or three years, a thirteenth month is included in order to make the months correspond with the movements of the earth around the sun. The years are named for the animals of the Chinese zodiac honoring each of twelve animals: horse, goat, monkey, rooster, dog, pig, rat, ox, tiger, rabbit, dragon, snake. According to ancient almanacs the most auspicious sign in the Chinese zodiac is the dragon. As in any zodiac, each person is born under a sign to which particular personal characteristics inhere. There are about 500,000 Chinese-Americans in the U.S. who celebrate their New Year on the 24th day of the 12th month. The arrival of the new year begins with fireworks, street parades, costumes, food, music and dancing. Though ten days to two weeks for public celebrations is popular, festivities may continue for as long as a month. Tourists come from all over to see the colorful celebrations in Chinese communities in San Francisco, Boston, Chicago, Los Angeles, New York and Honolulu. The best part is—you don't have to be Chinese to have a fun time.

Activities

1. Find your birth date on the Chinese zodiac chart. Find the animal sign which represents your year of birth. Follow up with some library research on Chinese horoscopes to determine if you are wonderful, clever and generous—recognize yourself? Or mean, selfish and sneaky (must be somebody else)!

2. Write your own dazzling Chinese horoscope: "I was born in the year of the snake . . . ." Write a horoscope for a relative born in a different year, under a different sign.

Animal Sign	Year of Birth			
Monkey	1968	1980	1992	2004
Rooster	1969	1981	1993	2005
Dog	1970	1982	1994	2006
Pig	1971	1983	1995	2007
Rat	1972	1984	1996	2008
Ox	1973	1985	1997	2009
Tiger	1974	1986	1998	2010
Rabbit	1975	1987	1999	2011
Dragon	1976	1988	2000	2012
Snake	1977	1989	2001	2013
Horse	1978	1990	2002	2014
Goat	1979	1991	2003	2015

GA1153

29. Chinese New Year

Chinese Zodiac

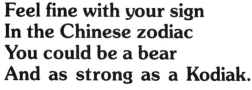

Feel fine with your sign
In the Chinese zodiac
You could be a bear
And as strong as a Kodiak.

So look at the horoscope
To make you feel good
Inflate your old ego
As horoscopes should!

The dog is as ever
An egalitarian
He loves the whole world
And all antiquarians.

The tiger is strong
With courage that shows
From the top of his head
To the tip of his toes.

The rat is well-known
For survival in history
His cunning and craft
Is surely no mystery.

The ox is dependable
And has a kind heart
Admired by all
For doing his part.

The dragon, a creature
Of mythical elegance
Who vanquished all royalty
He ever was up against!

So look for your sign
On your very own birthday
You'll see the Chinese
Have made it your worthday!

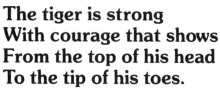

Greta B. Lipson

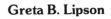

59

GA1153

Lesson 30: Snowflakes

The snow, which delights us when it first falls in early winter, is frozen water vapor. The flakes are formed in storm clouds where the temperature must be below freezing (32⁰ F). When a large number of flakes have formed, they tumble around and fall through the storm cloud. Some fall separately and some stick to others in their descent. A snowflake is an ice crystal, ". . . one of the most beautiful things in the museum of nature." Each flake has six arms or six sides, and no two flakes are ever alike. The countless beautiful designs depend upon particular conditions, such as temperature, height of clouds and the quantity of moisture in the clouds. The flakes are formed in an endless variety of geometric shapes: prisms, angles, points, feathers. Occasionally there are pictures in the newspapers of children romping in snow which they have never seen before. This is not surprising since it falls on only one third of the earth's surface. Truly exotic snow, which is red or green, is found in Greenland and the Arctic where, after the snow falls, the strange color change is affected by microscopic plants indigenous to the region. To study snowflake designs, let the snow fall on a dark sleeve or on a dark piece of cloth. Have a magnifying glass ready which will enable you to see the lacy patterns with greater clarity.

Activities

1. There is a form of patchwork poetry which is called "Cento."* It is made up of passages from assorted poetry which may or may not rhyme. For this project forget the rhyme scheme! Collect vivid lines of poetry about snow from a variety of poems. Put together your own cento poem. A group effort would be most interesting. Here is a start.

   "Soft as the fleeces of descending snow" by Homer
   "Try snow of heaven, heavy, soft, and slow" by G. Taggard
   "The fenceposts wear marshmallow hats" by Dorothy Aldis
   "Announced by all the trumpets in the sky, arrives the snow" by Ralph Waldo Emerson
   "Hold fast to dreams, for when dreams go Life is a barren field frozen with snow" by Langston Hughes
   "The moon wades deep in snow" by Elizabeth J. Coatsworth

2. Suggestion: Acquaint yourself with *Granger's Index to Poetry,* which is organized according to first lines of famous poetry. Find the subject index and look under "Snow."

---

*Greta B. Lipson and Jane A. Romatowski, *Calliope: A Handbook of 47 Poetic Forms and Figures of Speech* (Carthage, Illinois, Good Apple, Inc., 1981).

30. Snowflakes

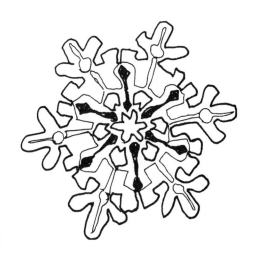

Winter Lace

Now are the snowflakes melting
Or will they touch the ground
So I can build a castle
That's icy, slick and sound.

The geometric jeweler
Who fashions these white gems
Enthralls me with His genius
With facets yet undreamt.

Greta B. Lipson

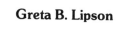

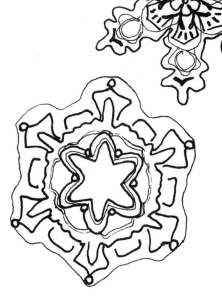

61

GA1153

Lesson 31: The Common Cold

One of the biggest nuisances of all, the common cold, is at its peak in the winter months. The cold, which can be as mild as a runny nose and as severe as bronchitis or pneumonia, is an infection of the mucous membrane lining of the nose. Colds are dangerous because they cause other serious illnesses as well. Unfortunately, one cold doesn't make you immune to other forms; in America alone it is calculated that there are countless illnesses caused by the common cold because they make the patient susceptible to other problems. Children are among the most frequent sufferers but, overall, colds keep more people away from school and work than any other illness. Absenteeism in turn costs billions in lost wages, lost time at work, medications and complications. Precautions against colds are not difficult to observe. When sneezing or coughing, a spray of moisture loaded with viruses that stay alive for days leaves the mouth. Cover your mouth when sneezing or coughing and spare others. People who refuse to stay home from school or work because they are Spartans do a great disservice to others with whom they come in contact. It is posited that colds are spread by hands. If you do have a cold—stay home—wash up—drink lots of fluids—and eat chicken soup!

Activities

1. Scientists have found hundreds of viruses that can cause the common cold. If you were a scientist and had to name these pesty little viruses, what would you call them? Remember—medical terms can be astonishing tongue twisters like *pneumoconiosis*. What cold remedies are used in your family?

2. Here is a funny art project guaranteed to tickle the funny bone. Use construction paper. Cut out a large oval for a face with stick-out ears. On a separate piece of construction paper, trace your hand and cut it out. Paste a cleansing tissue over the place for the nose on the face. Now paste (or staple) the hand over the tissue. Last, add the eyes, hair, freckles or anything to make the face look cartoony. Don't obscure the entire face with the tissue—leave room for facial features. Display these medical illustrations!

GA1153

31. The Common Cold

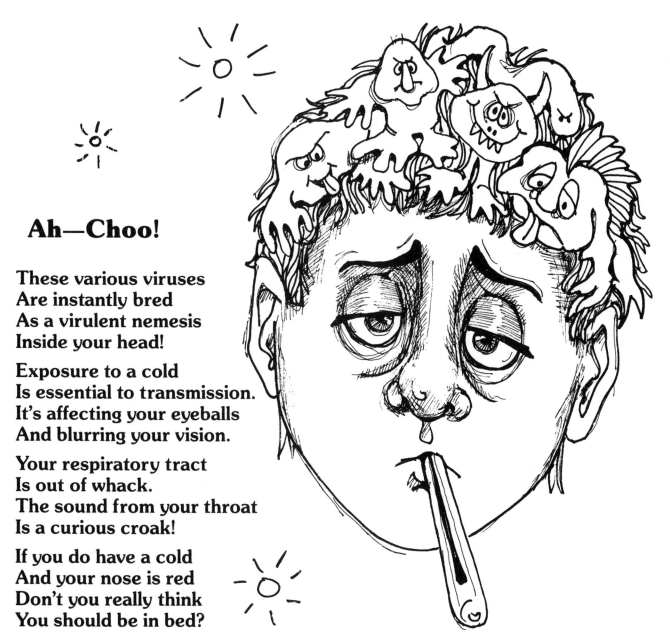

Ah—Choo!

These various viruses
Are instantly bred
As a virulent nemesis
Inside your head!

Exposure to a cold
Is essential to transmission.
It's affecting your eyeballs
And blurring your vision.

Your respiratory tract
Is out of whack.
The sound from your throat
Is a curious croak!

If you do have a cold
And your nose is red
Don't you really think
You should be in bed?

So do me a favor,
And close the door
'Cause discussing your symptoms
Is a horrible bore.

Greta B. Lipson

63

GA1153

Lesson 32: Black History Month

(Excerpted from a December, 1988 Michigan Education Association Bulletin, with permission.) "Carter G. Woodson, a black educator, historian and editor, is the father of Black History Month (formerly, Negro History Week, established in 1926). Woodson purposely selected the week which included Abraham Lincoln's birthday, February 12, and that of Frederick Douglass, February 14. Black History Month is a constant reminder that we have a long way to go before we achieve understanding of one another. Woodson knew that Blacks needed to know their history in order to be proud, as free men and women. He knew for certain that white people needed to understand the heritage of Blacks in order to help them to become integrated into the mainstream of American life. No racial, religious or ethnic group is without heroes. No racial, religious or ethnic group is without a heritage. It is when we share our heroes, our heritage and our cultures that we develop a true community. In its annual observance, Black History Month stresses past achievements and current accomplishments. It is important for all students to understand the tragic and difficult past of Blacks in America and the effects of past discrimination on this present generation. Only when Black History is given its appropriate place in the education of our young people . . . will we be able to build upon that foundation to insure that the land in which we live will foster social and economic liberty and justice for all."

Activities

1. To the teacher: For information, classroom materials and activities for Black History Month, write to your State or National Education Association—Professional Development Department.

2. *My Past Is My Own* aired on a CBS Schoolbreak Special on January 24, 1989, was an award-winning show about the civil rights struggle of the 60's. The film is available on video tape from Pyramid Film and Video, 2801 Colorado Ave., Santa Monica, CA 90404, (213) 828-7577. The material was scripted in a special CBS reading program newspaper sent out to schools. Questions regarding that publication should be addressed to: Director of Children's Programming, CBS, New York, NY, (212) 975-8778.

 GA1153

32. Black History Month

In Tribute to Black History

Affirm my pride in the history of my people,
Rejoice in our transcendental strength and courage,
Capture the quality that distills our fundamental essence.

Our quintessence
Given its full expression
Taps the stored honey
Of the Black soul.*

Distinction, imagination, panache.
In the conglomerate of all human beings
Our style sets us apart
And is indefinable.

We continue to endure.
With abiding strength and courage
We shall scale
The glass mountain.

The imprint and markings of our history
Have shaped our spiritual core, soul,
Marrow, sum and substance
Into that which is Black and different.

Greta B. Lipson

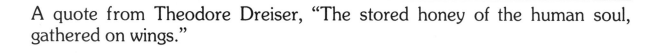

A quote from Theodore Dreiser, "The stored honey of the human soul, gathered on wings."

 GA1153

Lesson 33: Groundhog Day

On February 2, according to legend, the groundhog (a woodchuck) emerges from underground, where he has been hibernating all winter, to take a look around. If the sun shines and he sees his shadow, he becomes frightened and goes back into his hole. This is supposed to mean that winter will last six more weeks. If it is cloudy and the groundhog sees no shadow, he stays on the surface just lollygagging around. Weather lore claims that this is an indicator that spring will come early. The English and German immigrants brought to this country the custom of making a big fuss over the shenanigans of the groundhog. The media has successfully exploited this tradition. The first group observance, we are told, took place in Punxsutawney, Pennsylvania, in 1908. The folks there claim to reside in the "original home of the great weather prognosticator, His Majesty, the Punxsutawney Groundhog." Punxsutawney's Groundhog Club tramps to Gobblers Knob early in the morning of the big day to wait for the furry little fellow. The breakfast and dinners throughout the day include Woodchuck salad, Soothsayer gravy, Forecaster green beans and other gourmet delights. Everybody loves Groundhog Day, but don't look for it in a science book!

Activities

1. This is another test of humor for nonartists. Draw a picture of a February landscape on manila paper. Cut a hole in the paper at ground level. On another piece of paper, draw a brown furry groundhog with personality. Cut him out and glue him onto the top part of a Popsicle stick (or facsimile). Now place him in the picture by pushing him up through his hole in the ground and back down again. Behold your own weather predictor, and probably as accurate as a real live groundhog.

2. Finish this story: A groundhog just arrived at the surface on a February morning. It's sunny out—but before he scurries back into his hole, he sees a flower and figures he overslept and spring has already arrived. He's not too bright and does not recognize that the flower is artificial. He runs quickly to alert the animals and roust them out of their hibernation. His first stop is at the bear's sleeping place who opens up his bloodshot eyes to answer his doorbell . . .

33. Groundhog Day

What the Groundhog Doth Bring (Spring?)

Silly little thing
Does your shadow bring
Something that tells us
When we will have spring?

I don't believe a word of it!
That you were born
With so much wit
That you know what will bring the spring.

I raise my voice to contradict
That fuzzy groundhogs can predict
The weather.

I'll stick with folks who know the score
Who study the weather a whole lot more
Than groundhogs.

Greta B. Lipson

67

GA1153

Lesson 34: Thomas Edison's Birthday (1847-1931)

Thomas Alva Edison, nicknamed "The Wizard of Menlo Park," was born in Milan, Ohio, on February 11. His schooling in Port Huron, Michigan, did not start until he was seven. There was a mistaken notion that he was a slow child. The truth of this distortion was that Edison got along poorly with his schoolmaster who strapped students who asked too many questions. Soon Tom was in trouble with his teacher who reported to the school superintendent that the irksome boy was "addled." Edison's outraged mother removed him from school after a total of three months. This marked the end of his formal education. Edison was taught the basics at home by his mother. He soon became involved in whichever direction his intellect pulled him. By the age of 10, Edison had set up an efficient working lab in his basement. His curiosity generated strange probings and even stranger events. Once he sat on a basket of chicken and goose eggs to see if he could make them hatch. Another time, fascinated with flight, Edison gave his friend a triple dose of effervescing powder (used for indigestion) expecting that the accumulated gas in his friend's stomach would loft him into the air as a pre-flight phenomenon. Edison matured into a brilliant, prolific and eccentric genius who refused an operation for his deafness because he enjoyed the solitude it gave him. The stories of his life are legend. Edison patented 1093 inventions which have greatly affected the lives of people all over the world. Among these were the phonograph, the electric motor, the mimeograph, the telegraph and contributions to motion pictures. But his most remarkable invention, it is agreed, was the incandescent electric light bulb. Edison worked incredibly long hours, and when he heard himself described as a genius, he would say that genius was "two percent inspiration and ninety-eight percent perspiration."

Activities

1. If you would like to enter a competition for young inventors, write to: Invent America, U.S. Patent Model Foundation, 1331 Pennsylvania Ave., N.W., Suite 903, Washington, D.C. 20004, (202) 737-1836. This foundation offers more than $100,000 in prizes annually for pupils in grades k-8. Children are invited to enter their incentive ideas in a national contest. Perhaps you know someone who could use this information.

2. Try to imagine waking up to a world without the work of inventors. There would be no electricity, paper, refrigeration, cars, modern plumbing . . . Write a diary entry for one day in your life without civilization's greatest inventions. Start at 7 a.m.

34. Thomas Edison's Birthday

Incandescence

Most of the time he was in his lab
Seeing things others did not see
Pondering the imponderables.

He was looking for
    Something
    That would burn at high temps
    And create
    White light
    In a vacuum.

He tried everything
And then he discovered
    Tungsten.
    It heated up and
    As long as
    The current flow
    Was fixed
    It emitted a steady white light
    With little electrons coursing through
    The wires—forced toward
    A positive pole.

Now each of us can
Command a small switch on the wall
Make light burst into
A given space
Vanishing the darkness
Like a magic act.

Edison turned on the incandescent light bulb
And lit up our world!

Greta B. Lipson

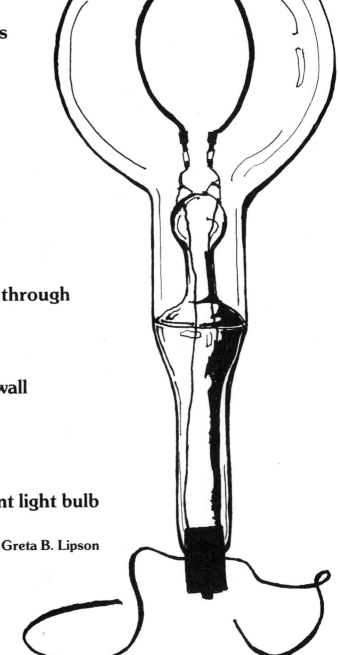

GA1153

Lesson 35: National Inventor's Day

This day is appropriately observed on Edison's birthday, and it is dedicated to the remarkable men and women who travel a circuitous track of discovery. "Things" are invented in response to a felt need, as in "Necessity is the mother of invention." The need may be at home, in business, industry, agriculture, medicine and technology; the list goes on. When a new device is invented it may function in ways never conceived by the inventor. It, in turn, may generate its own constellation of new ideas and demands. Sometimes, when we are rooted in old concepts, we are often not aware of the advantage of a more efficient possibility. When the telephone was invented, it was initially considered an interesting but not practical device. Who, but an inventor, could envision a better way to copy documents that would help revolutionize the world of information technology? Inventions help us save time and energy, help control the forces of nature, and improve the quality of life. But sometimes the technology of new frontiers has a down side that produces its own demons! The question of why people invent is a difficult one to answer since it involves the creative spirit, an irrepressible drive and the wonders of the human intellect. It is true that the monetary rewards of a successful invention are great, but financial motivation alone cannot account for the consuming dedication and intense work necessary to the realization of a new invention.

Activities

1. Be an inventor and draw a picture of a machine that will perform an important function for you (a "pick up the junk" in your room machine). Label the parts which may have names never heard of before. Write a TV commercial for your invention that will be an effective advertisement! Include the price.

2. Rube Goldberg was a clever cartoonist (1883-1970) who drew pictures of wild, wonderful complex machines that were designed to perform *very simple tasks*. An example of his genius was to create a machine that took twenty-five separate mechanical functions to crack open an egg! With the help of a reference librarian, locate information about college engineering fraternities all over the country that have competitions to keep the Rube Goldberg tradition alive! Could your class produce such a mechanical wonder with the help of a teacher or parent sponsor? See the book *The Best of Rube Goldberg*, compiled by Charles Keller © 1979, Prentice-Hall.

35. National Inventor's Day

A Whatchamacallit

To invent something
You need whirring wheels
Inside your head
And a different perspective
Of what you've read.

You need a venturesome soul
And intricate tools
With courage enough
To break the rules.

An idea itself
Is never enough
It's only a plan
That's in the rough

You're called an inventor
On one condition . . .
When you bring an idea
To its fruition!

And besides all that
It has always been said,
You need only want
To use your head!

Greta B. Lipson

Lesson 36: Abraham Lincoln's Birthday (1809-1865)

Abraham Lincoln was born in Kentucky on February 12. The young Lincoln was respected by his neighbors who recognized his qualities of leadership, elected him to the state legislature four times and later to Congress. Lincoln had profound convictions about justice for everyone. This conviction influenced his decision to become a lawyer despite his limited formal education of less than a year. Lincoln became active in national politics and, in 1861, when he was fifty-two years old, he became the sixteenth President of the United States. As the first President elected by the Republican party, Lincoln won the election with less than 40 percent of the popular vote. The Civil War, which tore the country apart, was ignited a year after his election. Lincoln was opposed to slavery which he denounced as a grievous wrong against humanity. He was steadfast in his determination to abolish slavery while preserving the Union and proving that democracy would prevail. The Civil War lasted four years, from 1861 to 1865. In 1862 Lincoln issued the Emancipation Proclamation; this paved the way for the adoption of Amendment 13 which ended slavery throughout the United States. Lincoln was then elected for a second term. One evening the tired President went to see a play at the Ford Theatre. Tragically, his life was ended by a shot fired by John Wilkes Booth. Americans mourned their "Father Abraham" who was buried in Springfield, Illinois, in Oak Ridge Cemetery—now a place of pilgrimage for those who cherish his humanity. Lincoln is known around the world for his nobility and dedication to the principles of equality and democracy.

Activities

1. Like many great men and women, Lincoln will forever be remembered for the power of his language. The Gettysburg Address was delivered at a ceremony held to dedicate a cemetery. Lincoln followed a "great" orator who had spoken for two hours. Lincoln spoke for only three minutes, but the audience was electrified. Locate the entire text of the Gettysburg Address in Bartlett's *Familiar Quotations*. Conduct a ceremonious class reading of the entire text: "Fourscore and seven years ago our fathers brought forth on this continent . . . ."

2. The press of Lincoln's time was purported to have been savage in their criticism of the Civil War President. Earlier, in Colonial times, Benjamin Franklin was one of the first to use the political cartoon as a weapon, which could shape public opinion as powerfully as the spoken word. Collect a week's worth of cartoons in the editorial section of your local newspaper. Analyze them in class for a point of view. How is ridicule used in some of the cartoons? Explain, "A picture is worth a thousand words." Do you believe that?

36. Abraham Lincoln's Birthday

Salute to Lincoln

Can you see greatness
In the face of a man—
The cares of his country,
The hope for our land,
The future for freedom,
The courage of man?

When I look at Lincoln,
I think that I can.

Greta B. Lipson

73   GA1153

Lesson 37: Valentine's Day

Valentine's Day started as a pagan fertility festival in ancient Rome to honor the wolf god Lupercus. The Christians later retained the holiday and re-dedicated it to a martyred Italian priest, St. Valentine, who died on February 14. The holiday became a time for exchanging gifts of sweets and flowers between sweethearts. Personal notes were sent, on which people drew hearts and flowers to enhance their expressions of love. Beginning in the 1400's, the holiday was observed in England and France with romantic superstitions to accompany the observance. (If you slept with bay leaves pinned to your pillow, a vision of your true love would appear in your dreams.) The English brought St. Valentine's Day to America. By the eighteenth century love notes were available commercially, and by 1840 the elegant, lacy, cupid-covered cards lay siege to the population. Just seven years later, Esther Howland, an enterprising woman in Worcester, Massachusetts, produced commercial valentines and in the first year sold three million sentimental notes. Today the greeting card business flourishes on February 14 as stores sell more than 485 million valentines a year. The candy makers are close behind, selling goodies in a volume ranking fourth behind Christmas, Halloween and Easter. Florists, too, cover America with ribbons and bouquets bearing messages of love. The modern observance has been expanded to include not only sweethearts, but all others. The commercial aspects of the holiday notwithstanding—any day is a good day to express friendship, love and loyalty.

Activities

1. Faithful friends are very important to us throughout our entire lives. Describe a friend you have (or would like to have) who means a great deal to you. What is there about this person that makes your relationship strong? What qualities does your friend have that you can characterize: a sympathetic listener, happy and optimistic, a good sense of humor, is generous and warm? Sometimes we are not sure what makes a friendship work well because we have never stopped to analyze it. Did the good chemistry work immediately or did it take time?

2. Make your own serious valentine or make a funny rebus valentine with the following greeting: Dearest one, I pine for you. Can you be my valentine?

Dearest **1**, 👁 🌲 **4** **U** . 🥫 **U** 🐝

my ❤ ?

37. Valentine's Day

Heart to Heart

Sometimes we wait
For a special day
To tell someone
In a special way
That friends mean a lot
If they're kind and true.

My valentine wishes
Say that to you!

Now you may think
That sounds overly mushy
And maybe even surprisingly gushy
But as always
I am quite self-controlled
About matters of import
That have to be told!

You're a buddy, a friend,
The best sort of pal
The best of the best
Of the boys and the gals!

Greta B. Lipson

75

GA1153

Lesson 38: Susan B. Anthony's Birthday (1820-1906)

Susan B. Anthony was born on February 15 in Adams, Massachusetts. This date is now celebrated as a time to acknowledge her unremittingly hard work on behalf of equality for women in the United States. Ms. Anthony was born into a Quaker family where equality for women was a tenet of her religion. Unfortunately, that view was not shared by the men who governed our country at that time and so American women did not have the same rights of citizenship as men. *Suffrage* means "the right to vote" and Susan B. Anthony devoted a lifetime to win that entitlement for women. Social change was badly needed: women could not own property; women were not allowed to sign wills; if women married, their money automatically became their husband's; women could not have custody of their own children. The abuses were manifold. Because Susan B. Anthony fought social injustice, she began to lecture widely urging the abolition of slavery. She experienced great frustration when she learned that among abolitionists there was no concern for the equal rights of women. Without the franchise to vote, women did not have the rights and privileges of men who were empowered to bring about social change. In 1870 Amendment 15 to the Constitution passed; the vote was given to black men but not to black women. It was clear that the battle lines for women of conscience were drawn. Ms. Anthony met Elizabeth Cady Stanton, and together they created a suffragist organization working exhaustively to win a women's suffrage amendment to the Constitution. Ms. Anthony remained president of the National Suffrage Association for eight years. Not until 1920, fourteen years after the death of Susan B. Anthony, did the nineteenth amendment to the Constitution become law—finally giving women the right to vote. So much that is taken for granted we owe to powerful suffragists—women of vision and courage who fought the battle for us.

Activities

1. The U.S. Treasury issued a Susan B. Anthony silver dollar in 1979 which was in circulation for only three years. The coin was the size of a quarter and was not widely used. It is now called a mini dollar and is fast becoming a prized collectible. Given this information you can probably design a better Susan B. Anthony dollar bill. Look at an authentic bill and then do your best.

2. What does it mean to be a "second class citizen"? Ms. Anthony was arrested and fined $100 for voting illegally (as a woman) in a presidential election in 1872.* Write a letter to the judge who fined her, expressing your opinion.

---

*Judith Papachristou, *Women Together: A History in Documents of the Women's Movement in the United States* (New York: Alfred A. Knopf, 1976).

GA1153

38. Susan B. Anthony's Birthday

Salute to Susan B. Anthony

Susan B. Anthony was:

A **S**talwart suffragist
Who was **U**ntiring in her efforts
to **S**ecure the vote
for all **A**merican women,
In a nation that declared all me**N** were created equal.

She was a **B**old fighter

Dedic**A**ted to the proposition that
Men and women alike were e**N**titled to the privileges
Of full ci**T**izenship and a voice
In the conduct of t**H**eir government
With equal access to **O**pportunity in
One nation u**N**der God
With libert**Y** and justice for all!

Greta B. Lipson

77

GA1153

Lesson 39: George Washington's Birthday (1732-1799)

George Washington was born in Westmoreland County Virginia. His family was wealthy and he grew up to be a prosperous plantation owner in Mt. Vernon. George Washington served his country in three important ways. As General Washington, he was the Commander-in-Chief of the Colonial armies during the Revolution. After the war, he was President of the Constitutional Convention in Philadelphia, where the laws were made that would bind the thirteen colonies together as one nation with a central government. Later, Washington answered the unanimous call of the people and was elected the first President of the Republic. He served from 1789 to 1796. Fortunately, for all Americans, after Washington's eight years as President (the last four years served reluctantly), he resisted the veneration of the public and went back home. In doing so he led the way for a peaceful transfer of power. Other revolutionary leaders in history, ". . .hundreds of them, generation after generation, named Napoleon and Castro, Zia and Mao, never went home; they had to be carried out, shot out or waited out." Thomas Jefferson, despite his serious rift with Washington, had a profound understanding of Washington's contribution to our democratic form of government. When Washington left office gracefully, Jefferson wrote: "The moderation and virtue of a single character probably prevented this revolution from being closed, as most others have been, by a subversion of that liberty it was intended to establish."*

Activities

1. Discuss the responsibilities of the presidency. Write a one-page paper or a paragraph that begins, "If I were President . . ." or "I would not want to be President because . . . ."

2. If you wanted to write to your U.S. senator or U.S. congressperson, to express an opinion, do you know what their names and addresses are?

---

*Based on an article by Richard Reeves, April 28, 1989, Other Voices Section, Op Ed., Detroit Free Press, United Press Syndicate. "In going home, Washington made history."

GA1153

39. George Washington's Birthday

Salute to Washington

(History tells us that following the victory of the Revolutionary War, some people wanted George Washington to become their king!)

Thank goodness his ego was not of a size
That would motivate him to want to reprise
The monarchy.

It was our good fortune
And infinite pleasure
To thank this man of
Heroic measure.

As a great commander
With no delusions
He came to the irrefutable conclusion
That Americans fought for democracy
Which would be our historical legacy.

He said:
"Listen to the people's voice,
And support the cause of political choice!
Throw off the shackles of monarchy
And declare your status as being free."

We said:
"As a sovereign people we proclaim your fame.
You are grand and glorious
Sweetly victorious
And history will extol your name."

Greta B. Lipson

79

GA1153

Lesson 40: Leap Year

If you were born on February 29, the pity is that you have a birthday only once every four years because—you were a leap year baby! February usually has only twenty-eight days in a year that normally has 365 days on the calendar. Therein lies the problem. The earth really takes longer than 365 days to complete its cycle around the sun. It actually takes five hours and forty-eight minutes longer to get around. Certainly something had to be done about this discrepancy between the calendar year and the solar year. The solution was to make the adjustment by adding an "intercalary" leap day every four years at the end of February! *Intercalary* simply means "added to the calendar." That change puts the calendar in harmony with the sun. It also gives the leap year 366 days. The leap occurs in every year that is divisible by four (1992-1996-2000-2004), except the years that mark the hundreds. A century can only be a leap year if it can be divided by 400, for example, 1600 and 2000. Having leaped over every fourth year, the calendar mavens are satisfied because they tell us that with this adjustment the calendar year and solar year will vary only one day in several thousand years. These events probably account for a great deal of mystery, superstition and leap year weirdness.

Activities

1. In the rich history of the calendar, it is clear that we owe a debt to the past, since the systematizing of time has helped the orderly conduct of human affairs. Imagine the entire city in a day without clocks or weeks without calendars. If it can be arranged with your teacher, try covering the wall clock in your room and disallowing watches for one complete day. Report the results.

2. For an interesting calendar experience, look in your school encyclopedia under "Calendar" and find something called a *perpetual calendar* which will give you exact days and dates for 277 years from 1753 to 2030. Do you want to know the day of Christmas when you were five-years-old? Or the day of your twentieth birthday? Or the day of the next family reunion on July 4th, five years from now? It's all there in the perpetual calendar! First study the calendar and then make a list of information you want to know.

40. Leap Year

Leap Year Blues

Do you see these tears
Streaming down my face?
'Cause in four long years
There's been no trace
Of my birthday!

Where's it been all this time?
How am I s'posed to know?
It's got me stymied,
Though I still grow
Without a birthday!

I have recently elected
To hire a detective
To look for my birthday
So I can have a mirthday
Like everybody else!

Greta B. Lipson

GA1153

Lesson 41: Women's History Month

Congressional Resolution
Designating the Month of March as
Women's History Month

Whereas American women of every race, class, and ethnic background helped found the Nation in countless recorded and unrecorded ways as servants, slaves, nurses, nuns, homemakers, industrial workers, teachers, reformers, soldiers and pioneers; and

Whereas American women have played and continue to play a critical economic, cultural and social role in every sphere of our Nation's life by constituting a significant portion of the labor force working in and outside of the home; and

Whereas American women have played a unique role throughout our history by providing the majority of the Nation's volunteer labor force and have been particularly important in the establishment of early charitable, philanthropic and cultural institutions in the country; and

Whereas American women of every race, class and ethnic background served as early leaders in the forefront of every major progressive social change movement, not only to secure their own right of suffrage and equal opportunity, but also in the abolitionist movement, the emancipation movement, the industrial labor union movement and the modern civil rights movement; and

Whereas despite these contributions, the role of American women in history has been consistently overlooked and undervalued in the body of American history:

Now, therefore, be it resolved by the Senate and the House of Representatives of the United States of America in Congress assembled, that the month of March is designated as "Women's History Month," and the President is requested to issue a proclamation calling upon the people of the United States to observe such month with appropriate ceremonies and activities.

Activities

1. It's time to let Betsy Ross and Florence Nightingale rest in peace! There are thousands of remarkable and accomplished women in the history of America. These women have made significant contributions to the greatness of our country, but their history has often been submerged and unaccounted for. Redress this wrong and start learning about them. For information and free materials, contact the National Women's History Project, 7738 Bell Rd., Windsor, California 95492, phone (707) 838-6000.

2. Find women in history of whom you have never heard, and research their accomplishments. Here are a few for starters: Amelia Earhart, Sarah Caldwell, Sojourner Truth, Harriet Beecher Stowe, Rachel Carson, Golda Meir, Rosa Parks, Sally Ride, Betty Freidan.

41. Women's History Month

In Praise of Forgotten Women

The task is clear—to celebrate the history of women
From deep in the past
In the arts and sciences
And in every endeavor in which women were permitted
(Or not permitted to participate because of their low status or no status).
But where are these women of substance?
Why are they invisible in written history?
Where are their markers
On the time line of civilization?
Where are the women who were artists, poets, musicians, scientists,
Doctors, midwives, inventors, writers, lawyers?
They did exist—but unrecorded,
Painted over, submerged, trivialized, of no consequence.
Because history records the story
Of the rich and powerful.
And long ago custom and law decreed
That women be denied social and political power.
But now society's code has yielded
As women seek equality
And look to the past
For insight and inspiration.

Greta B. Lipson

"We are entrusted with the lost legacy of women . . . To reclaim our past and insist that it become a part of human history is the task that lies before us, for the future requires that women, as well as men, shape the world's destiny."*

Judy Chicago (American artist)

---

*Excerpt from *The Dinner Party* by Judy Chicago, Copyright © 1979 by Judy Chicago. Used by permission of Doubleday, a division of Bantam, Doubleday, Dell Publishing Group, Inc.

Lesson 42: March Weather

On March 20 or 21 the sun is at the vernal equinox which is the time officially observed as the first day of spring. This is the month when we look for our first robin, when we see the crocuses and daffodils poke through the earth, when hibernating bears and woodchucks stir from winter sleep and when birds in heartening ritual fly north. March is the transition between winter and summer. It was revered by the ancients as a time when a female deity emerged from the winter darkness to create new life. The month of March is very strange, with characteristics of both winter and spring mixed together to make every day a surprise. There may be snowstorms and high winds in March or warm, sunny days with clear blue skies. The Romans named the month after Mars, the god of war, probably because March was so capricious and bad tempered. But Mars was also a protector of crops, so we are reminded that the new stirrings of life among plants and animals and birds begin to appear in this first month of awakening.

Activities

1. The first American almanacs that included weather sayings were printed before 1700. Many of these weather rhymes are still heard today. Can you find more? For example:

   - a January fog will freeze a hog
   - a sunny shower won't last half an hour
   - when smoke descends, good weather ends
   - evening gray and morning red, send the traveler wet to bed

   Now, can you make up some of your own for March or any other month?

2. Make an ongoing class list on butcher paper of weather words. How many words can you think of? How many weather symbols can you add? Look at the weather chart in your daily newspaper:

   misty, clear, penetrating, sweltering, humid, blustery, hot, balmy, smoggy, drizzling, hailing, pouring . . .

GA1153

42. March Weather

March Cryptogram

MA
RC hco ME
Sinl ik E ALi
ONA Ndg oe
So ut LI ke
A L A m B

Greta B. Lipson

GA1153

Lesson 43: Alexander Graham Bell's Birthday (1847-1922)

Alexander Graham Bell was an American inventor born in Edinburgh, Scotland, on March 3. His father, who had a strong influence on the boy, was a teacher of the deaf. The Senior Bell developed a physiological alphabet called "visible speech." Because Alexander was intensely interested in the problems of the deaf, he taught at Boston University as a professor of vocal physiology. In his lifetime he taught deaf people and the teachers of the deaf as well. Bell was determined to devise an electrical device which he hoped would help his students hear and assist them in learning to speak. He and his assistant, Thomas A. Watson, began work on the problem of sending the human voice over wires. One day, as each man was in a different room, Bell heard noises coming over Watson's transmitter to his receiver. Watson had accidentally completed the right circuit and the electric current had transmitted a sound to Bell. Soon after that episode the first intelligible words were spoken over the telephone, "Mr. Watson, come here, I want you!" Surprisingly, Bell was only twenty-nine years old when his patent for the telephone was granted in 1876. Bell, and two associates, Hubbard and Sanders, formed the Bell Telephone Company. The phone was first considered to be a cunning toy—but soon became a major part of modern living and changed the world. Bell continued to develop and invent, but once confided to his family that he would rather be remembered as a teacher of the deaf than as the inventor of the telephone.

Activities

1. This really does work. Bring in two tin cans with a small hole in the bottom of each can. Pass a long string through both cans and knot the strings on each end inside the cans. Choose a telephone partner—pull the string taut and stand far away from each other. Have a regular conversation using the cans as you would use a real telephone. Listen to your voices amplified.

2. If you have ever wanted to memorize a phone number, here's a useful trick to use. Your dial has groups of three letters assigned to each number:

   1. (Use the number as is)
   2. ABC
   3. DEF
   4. GHI
   5. JKL
   6. MNO
   7. PRS
   8. TUV
   9. WXY

   Make a real word, a nonsense word or a combination of letters and numbers from a phone number: 559-6489 spells "klynivy," 466-3269 spells "good boy." Try it and never forget a phone number again!

GA1153

43. Alexander Graham Bell's Birthday

Call Me, Ya Hear!

We made a telephone
Out of two tin cans,
And we pulled the string tight
With our own strong hands.

I can hear you talk
From your house far away
You can hear me, too.

What would Mr. Bell say?

Greta B. Lipson

GA1153

Lesson 44: Albert Einstein's Birthday (1879-1955)

Albert Einstein was born of Jewish parents in Ulm, Württemberg, Germany, on March 14. He was one of the intellectual giants of our time. His theory of general relativity revolutionized the field of physics in that it changed concepts of time, space, mass, motion and gravitation. When he was as young as fourteen years old, his speculations led him to ask the question, "How would the universe look if I were riding on a beam of light?" At twenty-one he graduated from his studies of mathematics and physics in Zurich and went to work as a clerk in a Swiss patent office where the solitude gave him time to work on his doctorate. He contributed scientific papers which were fundamental to the field of quantum mechanics. He received the Nobel prize in 1921. In 1933 the Nazi government launched its oppression of the Jews at which time the Germans took away Einstein's property, his academic rank and his German citizenship. He soon accepted a lifetime position at the Institute for Advanced Study in Princeton, New Jersey, where he stayed until his death at the age of 75. The great scientist had a grave concern that his physics theories would be used to develop weapons of destruction. Indeed, his worst fears became a reality. The release of atomic energy laid the foundation for the atomic bomb in 1945 and later the hydrogen bomb. Einstein was deeply religious, though he had no formal ties to organized religion. He was a man given to deep philosophical thought and compassion for humanity. Out of great reverence for the absolute laws and order of the universe, he believed "a legitimate conflict between science and religion cannot exist. Science without religion is lame; religion without science is blind."*

Activities

1. If it is true that at high velocities time slows down, this could cause a dislocation under some circumstances. Assume that you were sent into space on a scientific mission. The aging process was slowed down because of the speed of your spacecraft. When you arrived home you were younger, by thirty years, than your peers. Describe this strange turn of events to the class.

2. Investigate a contest called Odyssey of the Mind conceived by Samuel Micklus, a college professor in Glassboro, New Jersey. It is designed to teach creativity to kids in kindergarten through college. Schools become members in order to participate. The curriculum materials are contributed by IBM. The annual competition celebrated its tenth anniversary in 1989, boasting a total of 350,000 kids, including international participants.**

*Abraham Pais, *Subtle Is the Lord: The Science & Life of Albert Einstein* (Oxford University Press, 1982).

**See *Encyclopedia of Organizations.*

GA1153

44. Albert Einstein's Birthday

Relatively Speaking, Mr. Einstein

Admire smart people?
Here's a hero to lionize,
The great Albert Einstein
Had a mind to idolize.

Ideas are a legacy
So work hard to sustain
Your best investment,
Which is your brain!

Use your intellect
And mental capacity
To intersect thoughts
With sharp audacity.

Whether you're Einstein
With cerebral intensity,
A Smith, Jones or Feinstein
Could have that propensity!

So—press onward and upward
The way you've been taught
To higher and higher
Levels of thought!

Greta B. Lipson

89

GA1153

Lesson 45: Anniversary U.S. Standard Time Act

On March 19, 1918, Congress passed the Standard Time Act, which also established Daylight Saving Time. In the old days there were problems with clock time because every little town and hamlet was content to establish its own sun time ("Every place on earth that is east or west of another place has noon at a different time.") We can only imagine the confusion created for train schedules and travellers beyond the city limits. England was one of the first countries to solve the problem of "local" time. In 1850 the British standardized time according to the sun time at Greenwich, England, located on the prime meridian. Greenwich time became known as standard time, thus solving the problem neatly for the relatively small areas of England, Scotland and Wales. This would not work for America because of its greater size. The natural sun time in America was too variable over a distance of 3000 miles from the East Coast to the West Coast. The sun rises in New York but does not rise in California until three hours later. The successful plan to make standard time work in the U.S. divided the country into four time zones in the continental United States: Eastern Standard Time, Central Standard, Mountain Standard, and Pacific Standard. The local sun time in the middle of each zone was used as the standard time for the entire zone. There is one hour difference between each of the standard time zones in the continental United States. When it is 4 p.m. Eastern time, it is 3 p.m. Central time; 2 p.m. Mountain and 1 p.m. Pacific time. The states of Alaska and Hawaii are in their own zones. The innovation of Daylight Saving Time was introduced during World War I to save energy and is still observed today. To avoid confusion about when Daylight Saving begins and ends, try using this memory aid: spring forward, fall back! Daylight Saving begins the last Sunday in April and ends the last Sunday in October.

Activities

1. For a clear picture of time zones, consult the front pages of your telephone directory where you will find an excellent map of the U.S. which indicates area codes and time zones across the country from Eastern time to Pacific time and more. Draw four clocks and indicate the correct time on each starting with 4 p.m. in New York. Start from the East Coast to the West.

2. During Daylight Saving Time the clocks are set ahead one hour, which gives an added hour of daylight recreation in spring and summer. If a state prefers, it may remain on standard time by legislative vote. Based on this information, design a tricky traveler's time question for the class to solve. Example: You depart New York City at 3 p.m. E.S.T. for a three-hour flight to San Francisco. What is your arrival time? Answer: 3 p.m.

45. Anniversary U.S. Standard Time Act

Ticktock

He moves his hands
Around his face
From 1 to 12
From place to place.

The numerals that
They're touching say
The time it is
In night or day.

I don't believe
In being a slave
To anything
That won't behave.

And clocks can be
A mean taskmaster
When I am slow
And they move faster!

Greta B. Lipson

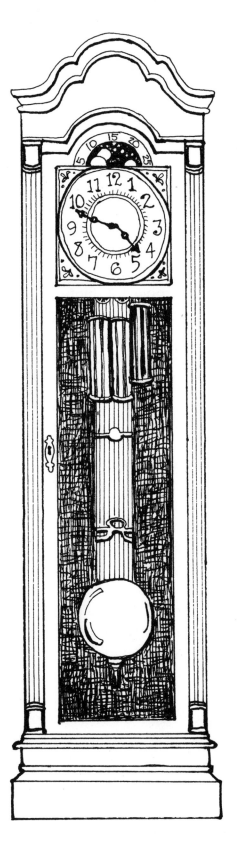

GA1153

Lesson 46: Kite Festivals

Kites were invented sometime between 400 and 300 B.C. in Greece. Kites have since been flown, with unflagging interest, all over the world by children and adults. Spring, when the winds blow hard, is a most popular time for kite flying and the time when kites do some of their fancier sailing. Many of these beauties can be seen on the beach which is a favorite place to catch vigorous winds in a totally clear area. Kites are appropriately named after the kite bird which is a member of the hawk family and is an extraordinarily graceful glider. All over the country there are exciting competitions where kites are judged for the most artistic, the trickiest maneuvers, the most responsive and other such characteristics. Kites have been used in many fields of endeavor: war, science, construction, photography, flight, meteorology, radio transmission and more. Flying kites for their sheer beauty is a very old and popular sport. The most startling performance is created by people with skill and a good pair of gloves, who achieve the necessary angle for flight called "angle of attack." One of the best-known experiments with a kite was performed by Benjamin Franklin in 1752 when he flew a silk kite in a thunderstorm to prove that lightning and electricity were the same thing. For hundreds of years some of the most breathtaking kite festivals have taken place in Asian countries. At these colorful events, thousands of kites in the shapes of dragons, birds, fishes and butterflies fill the sky. Most notable of these festivals is the Chinese Kites' Day and the Japanese Boys' Festival where carp kites flying in the air look like fish swimming upstream with open mouths. The carp, a good luck fish, is made for every Japanese boy in the family as part of the symbolism of this traditional festival. There is a term in Japan for people who are wild for kites which translates into "kite crazy."

Activities

1. Think about this question and decide carefully. When you have given your answer, you will join one of two groups whose members agree with you for purposes of further discussion. "What would you rather be—the kite or the string?" Why? If you change your mind, you may go over to the other side. Who persuaded you to change your point of view?

2. As a matter of common sense, list some rules in the kite-flying code: Do not fly a kite in a thunderstorm; do not use wire or wet string; never attach metal to a kite; stay away from electrical wires and avoid streets. If your kite becomes entangled in high wires or a tree, do not try to retrieve it!

GA1153

46. Kite Festivals

Kite in Flight

Fly that kite,
High as you please.
Into the sky,
Over the trees.

Fill it with wind,
Color with sun.
Let out the string,
And run, run, run!

Greta B. Lipson

93

GA1153

Lesson 47: Saint Patrick's Day

Every year the Irish people observe St. Patrick's Day in honor of the patron saint of Ireland who died on March 17 in the year 385 A.D. There are many legends about the kindly bishop, St. Patrick, and what he did for Ireland, but we are not sure how many of these stories are true. It is more certain, however, that St. Patrick made an important contribution to learning. Most people of his time were without any education, but St. Patrick taught all the people he baptized how to read and write. The Irish were then among the few people who could pass on these literacy skills to their children and they in turn to future generations. On St. Patrick's Day it is an ancient custom to wear a green shamrock or a bit of green to celebrate the day of the Irish. The shamrock seen on so many lapels is a graceful little three-leaf clover which is the national flower of Ireland. Though in America we are not all Irish, many of us, since 1737 have joined in the fun and helped our friends celebrate the holiday, too! An annual St. Patrick's Day Parade has taken place on Fifth Avenue in New York City as a charming tradition. The parade currently lasts six hours, includes 125,000 marchers, has a two-and-one-half-mile route passing St. Patrick's Cathedral and boasts vendors who sell refreshments, hot dogs and assorted treats dyed green!

Activities

1. A Blarney Stone is a stone in Blarney Castle in the county of Cork, Ireland. It is said to impart skill in blarney to those who kiss it. Blarney is smooth talk used to compliment, flatter or turn the head of the listener. Some examples could be: "You have the biggest muscles of any boy I've ever seen." or "You're the most understanding teacher I've ever had." or "No one in the whole world understands me like you do!" Manufacture some blarney of your own.

2. Make a huge green shamrock folder from construction paper. To make a shamrock, cut out three hearts and paste them together with a stem. On the front, write *Erin Go Bragh* which means "Ireland forever." All around the shamrock, write all the words the class can brainstorm that are connected to St. Pat's Day, such as *harps, green, pipes, shillelaghs, shamrocks* and *Emerald Isle.* Paste the poem inside the folder.

94

GA1153

47. Saint Patrick's Day

You Don't Have to Be Irish

Wear it bright,
Wear it well.
Wear it green
On your lapel.

Irish all—
Just today.
Shamrock's say,
"Saint Patrick's Day!"

Greta B. Lipson

95

GA1153

Lesson 48: Maple Sugar Time

Maple sugar is produced chiefly from the sap of sugar maple trees, though the black, silver and red maple trees are also used. The seeds of these trees are carried in the graceful wing pods that fly so well in the wind. The sap flows in the trees in the late winter until the middle of April. To secure the sap, a hole 1½″ deep is bored into the trunk of the tree. A tube or spout is forced into the hole and a pail is hung from the spout. The sap drips into the pail, which is covered for cleanliness, then is collected and taken to the sugarhouses to be boiled in large kettles or an evaporator. The watery, slightly sweet sap is boiled until some of the water evaporates and it becomes syrupy. This product is delicious maple syrup. If the sap boils longer, the end product will be maple sugar. Maple syrup is more expensive than other syrups, because it is produced in small quantities. It takes about forty gallons of sap to produce one gallon of syrup. The commerical production of maple sugar is an important business in New York, Ohio, New England and eastern Canada. While the term *sugaring off* refers to the process of cooking the sap, it also describes the happy gatherings the farm families have during maple sugar time.

Activities

1. Situated on your farm is a little home style restaurant called the Gingerbread House. You want to create a breakfast and lunch menu that emphasizes maple sugar delights. Offer your patrons anything you can think of that could possibly use maple syrup. Use noun clauses and lots of adjectives in your descriptions. Read your yummy menu aloud. For example:

   - light-as-a-feather pancakes topped with buttery syrup
   - hearty French toast with hot maple syrup
   - stick-to-your-ribs oatmeal with a sweet syrup glaze
   - down-home nourishing grits with bubbly syrup

2. A metaphor is a figure of speech which compares two unlike things with no words of comparison (like, as . . .). Write a *sweet* metaphor: Kisses are candy. Then add three or four short descriptive phrases to produce a short metaphor lyric!

Kisses are candy	A marshmallow hug
A sweet present	Downy velvet
Wrapped with care	Soft and pure
Lots of flavors	Puffs up my heart
Yummy and delicious	With sweet affection

   Make this a group project. Start with a metaphor and add four more lines. Which group can produce the fastest and the best metaphor lyric?

GA1153

48. Maple Sugar Time

To the Sugarhouse, Please

The sap is running
In the sugar maple trees.
Take the sap in the pails
To the sugarhouse, please.

Boil forty gallons,
Cook it all with ease,
Make some maple syrup
For my pancakes, please!

Greta B. Lipson

97

GA1153

Lesson 49: April Fool's Day

April Fool's Day or All Fools' Day has always been observed on the first day of April. This is the time for people of all ages to play jokes on one another while trying hard to be convincing. The April fool custom is so old that its ancient origins are uncertain; some people believe it began in ancient Rome as part of a pagan celebration of the vernal equinox. There is further evidence that it was celebrated for the first time in India, as part of their spring festival called Huli, which marks the end of the month of March. During Huli people are sent on nonsensical errands and tricked into believing foolish pranks. A charming account of April Fool's Day has its beginnings in France with the reign of Charles IX in 1564 when the King adopted a new calendar that changed New Year's Day from April 1 to January 1. Some diehards refused to observe the new calendar and so were called April Fools! By the 1600's it was widely adopted, and it became fashionable to fool friends in April. This lighthearted custom was observed in eighteenth century England and then moved on to America. So take care. Because if you are duped on the first of April, you might feel ridiculous and may be called a fool, an April gawk or a cuckoo, as the Scottish folks say.

Activities

1. Recall the funniest trick that was ever played on you at any time. It need not have occurred on April Fool's Day. Unfortunately, we can be made to feel foolish at any time of the year. Find your courage and be honest about the anecdote. It's not easy to admit to being as dense as a turnip! If it's less embarrassing, ask the teacher to read written accounts of these experiences as if they were anonymous.

2. Tall tales are different than other humorous stories because tall tales are characterized by the most outrageous exaggeration. You would have to be a fool to believe these yarns. Read about a folk hero of your choice and recount some of the ways in which the stories stretch the truth. Find tall tales about Paul Bunyan, Pecos Bill, Davy Crockett and Daniel Boone for starters. Have a tall tale storyfest to celebrate April Fool's Day.

GA1153

49. April Fool's Day

Just an April Fool

April fool—you better watch
The ditzy tricks we play!
We'll laugh at all the weird jokes
We play on you today.

We'll shout at you
Your pants are split!
Your dog just flew away!
Your hair is blue!
Your teeth are green!
This crazy April day!

Now be a sport
And don't get mad
No matter what we do.
Just turn your hairy ears this way.
For a friendly word or two:

    Hold your tongue
    Look real cool
    Don't get mad,
    When we say you drool!
    Don't let it faze you
    Nor should it craze you
    'Cause soon April one will be April two!

(You really are a good egg! So whatsa matter—can't you take a yolk?)

Greta B. Lipson

GA1153

Lesson 50: Easter Rabbit

Rabbits, chicks, eggs and lilies are among the many symbols which celebrate Easter when people see an unfolding of the cycle of life beginning anew. The Easter rabbit tradition comes from Germany, where the children built nests in which the bunny would "lay" beautifully colored eggs to be found on Easter morning. In the world of make-believe the favorite rabbit seems to be a replica of the cottontail rabbit which is the most common found in the U.S. The mother (doe) and father (buck) each have an engaging fluffy tail like an attached powder puff, which accounts for their popularity. In real life there are many types of rabbits, both wild and tame, all over the world. They are all known for their long ears and their speed which protects them from their enemies. Rabbits do not walk but instead move by leaping or hopping as fast as eighteen miles an hour. They make their homes in fields and prairies where in a year they produce an average of several litters, with about three to six in a litter. Count that up and you have as many as eighteen babies a year. Rabbits are vegetarians, which is a good thing to be, but their eating habits cause farmers a great deal of trouble, which is bad!

Activities

1. In the Easter spirit of finding things carefully hidden—track down the incredible picture book, *Masquerade*, by Kit Williams, © 1979. The English author-artist actually hid a $6000 jeweled rabbit pendant set with turquoise, moonstones and rubies. Williams included clues in his picture book to help searchers find the precious necklace. The scavenger hunt took three years, during which time people from all over the world, in their quest for the necklace, were digging holes all over England. The jewelled piece was found in a Bedfordshire village thirty-five miles north of London. The rabbit pendant is currently worth $36,000. You may not believe this story, but it is true. Find the article in *Newsweek* magazine, March 29, 1982, issue, page 36.

2. Randy Rabbit's Junk Food Hall of Shame! Help the cause of healthful eating. Put up a piece of white butcher paper in the room. Each student will participate by adding to a list of the names of popular junk foods. Read the labels and wrappers. Include the preposterous sounding ingredients to your list. Research some of the chemicals used in these foods.

50. Easter Rabbit

Health Food Habit Rabbit

His fur is white
His nose is pink
But no one asks him
What he thinks
(about candy).

He likes lettuce and cabbage
And other good stuff
But jelly beans and chocolate creams
Are terribly rough
(on his stomach).

So take his lead for healthy eats
And shop in a store
Where they have more
(than junk food treats).

'Cause Easter bunnies
And ordinary rabbits,
As a furry group,
Have good eating habits
(and nutrition).

Greta B. Lipson

GA1153

Lesson 51: Easter Eggs

Historically the egg has represented fertility and life. It was the Persians and Egyptians who first exchanged eggs that were painted in fragile hues of springtime. Later, the Christians exchanged colored eggs as an expression of the joyous Resurrection. The custom survived and by 1880 the English were making irresistible chocolate eggs with charming cutout windows, interior scenes and dated messages. Throughout history decorated eggs have been prized gifts, as exemplified by the folk art tradition of painting eggs called Psyanky. This art form is common in the Ukraine and in most other Eastern European and Baltic countries. These eggs are characterized by geometric patterns executed in bold, dramatic colors. There is a legend which cautions that if the tradition of Psyanky should stop, a chained monster would be unleashed to devour the world! Among other Easter traditions brought to America was the custom of egg-rolling, a practice which was officially adopted by President Madison in 1809. This delightful event takes place every Easter Monday on the White House lawn, where grown-ups are allowed only if accompanied by a child. All children under twelve bring their own hard-boiled eggs and on signal, roll the eggs down the grassy slope! (This practice may be symbolic of the stone that was rolled away from Christ's tomb on Easter morning.)

Activities

1. For a language challenge, think of as many egg or egg-related sayings as you can that you have heard. These sayings may be idioms, proverbs or substitutions.

   - I like him 'cause he's a good egg (idiom).
   - He's got egg on his face (he's embarrassed).
   - Don't count your chickens before they hatch (egg related).
   - An egg a day keeps the doctor away (substitution).
   - Don't put all your eggs in one basket (proverb).

2. Make an Easter egg tree. Fill a bucket with sand or cement which can be purchased from a lumberyard. Find some sturdy, graceful branches. Force them securely into the sand. Spray-paint the branches with any choice of color. Use any commercial containers or cartons that resemble eggs. Paint them and use metallic string or yarn to attach to the eggs to hang from the branches. The tree will enjoy a long life.

GA1153

51. Easter Eggs

All Grades in Rainbow Shades

Dip your brush in a rainbow
Colors flow full of light.
Paint to capture the springtime,
Easter eggs for delight.

Greta B. Lipson

103

GA1153

Lesson 52: Spring Rain

Rain, so vital to life, develops in the never-ending process of evaporation. The sun makes the air warm, and the warm air rises and takes with it moisture from the land and sea. This moisture cannot be seen because it travels upward in the form of water vapor. The moisture-laden air cools as it rises and forms a cloud which contains millions of tiny droplets of water. When air cools to a particular degree (the dew point), the cloud can no longer hold any more moisture and it produces rain which falls to the earth. And so the process of the water cycle continues. Moisture from the earth is continually carried upward by the wind and eventually comes back down again in the form of precipitation. All growing things—plants, animals and humans—depend upon rain as a necessity of life. For all these reasons, the problem of acid rain, which is a product of pollution, is a serious issue. Acid rain includes all precipitation (rain, snow, sleet). When a car is started it gives off gases into the atmosphere. So do factories, power plants and other sources that burn such fuels as coal, gasoline and oil. When these gases mix with water particles in clouds, they form acids such as sulfuric acid and nitric acid. When the water particles fall to the earth as rain, they are much more acidic than normal, adversely affecting lakes, rivers, streams and water life all over the world. Because dry acid deposits may also reach the earth as significant pollutants, the term *acid deposition* includes both wet and dry forms. Damage is also done to buildings, bridges, forests and animal life. Crops and soil weakened by acid rain are more susceptible to disease. Everyone can help reduce the problem of acid rain by using less energy which produces pollutants.

Activities

1. Of all the things that are universally shared, a rainy day "mope" is a mood we have all experienced. Write a *mood piece* about how you feel on a grey, rainy day, when it's wringing wet outside. For a dynamite inspiration, locate a tape or record of environmental sounds. You can listen to a recorded rainy day as you write.

2. Research more information on acid rain. How does our use of energy create this problem and what can each individual do about it? Collect data under the heading of "Facts and Solutions." Bring your list to class and exchange information. Remember to cite the source. Include titles of books or articles—author, date, publisher and page number—as a good researcher would.

52. Spring Rain

April Rain

Ask me how I love the rain.

I love it like the flowers do.
Like grass and buds
And all the new things who
Feel themselves grow and come alive
In spring.

Rain makes it true.
Ask me how I love the rain.

Greta B. Lipson

GA1153

Lesson 53: Arbor Day

Arbor Day has enjoyed a resurgence because of the growing concern about loss of forests, expansion of deserts, acid rain and air pollution. Trees are critical to our lives because the green leaves add oxygen to the air we breathe while removing carbon dioxide and other pollutants. What is more, trees help prevent the greenhouse effect which is the excessive heating of the atmosphere, a condition which is causing international anxiety. As a start, the American Forestry Association launched a campaign to plant 100 million trees in U.S. cities by 1992. We are told that to reverse the greenhouse effect, it will take the planting of one trillion trees in the next twenty years. Trees are not only beautiful to look at but, during the summer, the sun blocked by one tree can cool your house equal to the performance of five air conditioners running for twenty hours. In winter, evergreens can also protect your house by breaking the force of the wind and reducing heating bills as much as 20 percent. Trees also improve the quality of our lives as the "lungs and thermostat of our planet." We are indebted to J. Sterling Morton, a resident of Nebraska, the "Tree Planter's State," who headed a movement in 1871 to protect the land by conserving the trees. Trees protect the soil and are essential to all living things. Interestingly, trees continue to grow as long as they stand, which may be for twenty years or for centuries. This fact is one of the reasons that people conscious of the gifts of nature feel great distress to see trees destroyed irresponsibly.

Activities

1. Make plans for an Arbor Day observance well in advance. Sponsor the purchase of a tree for your school. To raise funds organize a *used* book sale in your classroom. Put out a call to parents for donated used books suitable for children and adults. Decide on one price for hard covers and one price for paperback books. Invite all the students and neighbors (on a scheduled time plan) to browse and make purchases. Contact a tree nursery when your profits are accounted for and have a tree planting ceremony on April 26.

2. Environmentalists warn that cutting down the Amazon rain forest threatens the global climate and "the greatest repository of life on the planet." Find out why this destruction is taking place by doing library research. (Answer: The Brazilian government sees the rain forest as a source of wealth—as do loggers, ranchers, gold miners, industrialists and poor people who are clearing the land to farm, as the last frontier.)

GA1153

53. Arbor Day

The Greening of the Planet

It was a tender, tiny tree,
And we planted it with care—
A shy and skinny seedling
That shivered in the air.

We watered it and worried.
We did our very best—
And now its graceful beauty
Tells us nature did the rest.

Greta B. Lipson

107

GA1153

Lesson 54: Law Day

The American Bar Association is reponsible for the concept of Law Day which became an official national observance under President Kennedy in 1961. Law Day is a time to underscore the role of law in a democracy. Law forms the foundation of civilization and rests on the bedrock premises of justice and fairness. In the United States there is an added requirement for laws. In our country and other democracies, laws are made by the people or by representatives elected by the people. That single fact separates free societies from totalitarian forms of government. Because democracies rely on the will of the people, there is a special responsibility placed on citizens to participate in that government. To participate effectively, it is incumbent upon citizens to be educated about the issues of the day and the way their government works. The purpose of Law Day is to acknowledge the role of law in our nation: "to foster respect for law; to increase public understanding of the place of law in American life . . . ." There are countless Law Day exercises that take place all over the country on May 1. These are sponsored by more than 1400 state and local bar associations in conjunction with schools, churches, public service organizations, businesses and industries.

Activities

1. Discuss the statement: "Law touches our lives from the day of our birth to the day we die—from birth certificate to death certificate!"* Trace the presence of law in your life. Don't forget anything. Start from the moment you are born in a hospital.

   a. Birth certificate
   b. Licensed hospitals
   c. Physicians and nurses with college degrees
   d. Pharmacists with degrees
   e. American citizenship of baby
   f. Registered car, licensed driver
   g. Neighborhood city services
   h. Schools (legally enforced attendance)

2. Why do you think we need laws? What would daily life be like without laws? Invite an attorney or a law student to your classroom on Law Day. Ask about the presumption of innocence in the American legal system— "...innocent until proven guilty"—and ask her/him to discuss "due process" which is a constitutional right that requires a fair hearing before one can be punished. It is always courteous and productive to have a planned session with organized questions for a guest who is kind enough to visit and speak with the class.

---

*Greta B. Lipson and Eric B. Lipson, *Everyday Law for Young Citizens* (Carthage, Illinois: Good Apple, Inc. © 1988).

54. Law Day

Rules Rule

WITHOUT THE LAW
It would be a jungle out there with people swinging from vines.

WITHOUT THE LAW
Nobody could make you go to school because there wouldn't be one.
You could just hang around the cave all day and get dumber every minute.

WITHOUT THE LAW
The strong ones would beat up the small ones and nothing would be fair.

WITHOUT THE LAW
Dishonest people could steal the things for which you worked hard
And nobody would give a hoot.

WITHOUT THE LAW
There wouldn't be a government, with freedom of speech
Or freedom of religion
Or freedom of the press
Because wild people would be growling and throwing stones at one another instead.

WITHOUT THE LAW
There wouldn't be education or science or technology or justice or commerce.
Instead, people would keep busy painting stick figures on cave walls.

WITHOUT THE LAW
Our existence would be filled with insecurity and fear.

SO THINK ABOUT PROTECTING THE GIFT OF LAW IN YOUR LIFE—
OR YOU MIGHT FIND YOURSELF HUDDLED AROUND A FIRE,
SHAKING A RATTLE TO KEEP EVIL SPIRITS AWAY!

Greta B. Lipson

Lesson 55: May Day

You may ask, "What's so hot about May Day?" (Forgive the pun.) But the day includes a diverse range of activities, not the least of which are the annual school May festivals. Celebrations can be traced to the ancients who appreciated the month as a time when the chill of early spring has passed and the world is in bloom. May Day is a balmy hiatus before the rigors of summer heat. The European observance started with the Romans who would celebrate with parades, singing and dancing to honor Flora, the goddess of flowers. Other celebrants might choose to dance around newly awakened trees that were bursting with May blossoms—a ritual which was a vestige of the tree worship of the Druids. Later came the fanciful custom of dancing around the maypole while clutching its streaming multi-colored ribbons. In medieval England, May Day was an important public holiday when everyone went "a-Maying" and brought back boughs and garlands of blossoms to decorate the villages. A superstition of the time held that a face washed in the dew of a May morning would be instantly transformed in beauty. If you were lucky, on the eve of May Day you might find, left as a sign of affection, a May basket hanging on your doorknob. If the May Day celebration in America is muted, it is attributable to the influence of the Puritans. They disapproved of a holiday observance which included dancing and singing. But then—everybody did not sing on May Day. In America in the 1890's, the first of May was a time to demonstrate in support of the struggle of organized labor for an eight-hour working day. Later it became a day for labor demonstrations in Europe. In Russia and other Communist countries, it is a national holiday celebrated with political speeches and military parades.

Activities

1. Write an unrhymed poem about May. Entitle it "Listening to May." Find a peaceful place to sit outside of school. Listen carefully to all the sounds you hear. Write short phrases about the sounds and your feelings as you listen. End your poem with a summary statement. For example:

   Trees rustle softly
   I hear a bird calling
   Laughter floats out the school window
   The breeze bends new flowers
   Sunshine warms my face
   Nature whispers to me.

2. May Day includes the observance of the progress of the labor movement in America. These gains also govern child labor laws which vary from state to state. Write to your State Labor Department to find out what you need to do officially to be employed as a minor.

GA1153

55. May Day

Bowers of Flowers in May

Ahhh . . .
The wonders OF
The certainty OF
Those vernal multi-colors OF
Flowers and blooms
And blossoms and buds
Of May Day!

In clusters and crowds and
Bunches and sprays
Voiceless
Yet clamoring
Pretty turned up faces
Of oodles and caboodles of flowers
On May Day!

Brilliant, dramatic
Docile and demure. Thorny and
Aggressive. Winning and
Fragile. Big and boisterous
And heart-wrenchingly gorgeous
Are flowers on
May Day.

Welcome May Day
With your
Ineffably beautiful
Amplitudinous,
Variegated
Springtime bouquet!

Greta B. Lipson

111

Lesson 56: Cinco de Mayo

Cinco de Mayo, translated from Spanish, means "the fifth of May," which is a national holiday in Mexico. This date marks the anniversary of the Battle of Puebla in 1862 in which the Mexicans, under the leadership of General Ignacio Zaragoza, defeated the French. More momentous than the victory were the circumstances of the battle against the forces of Napoleon III. In the face of an imperious enemy—outnumbered three to one, the Mexican soldiers emerged the victors. Understandably the battle had implications far beyond the events of the day. It represented the achievement of the indomitable human spirit. The events leading up to the battle started with Mexico having defaulted payments on bonds to France, Spain and England. The three countries made a naval demonstration against Mexico in order to force payment from Mexico. But after the others sailed for home, Napoleon had plans of conquest. It was Napoleon's tide of power that the Mexicans resisted. On the fifth of May the victory so reinforced their morale that they won the day and ultimately their freedom from the possibility of French domination. Cinco de Mayo is widely observed by Mexicans and friends everywhere with parades, festivals, dancing and speeches. An endearing characteristic of Americans is our eagerness to participate in the richness of the ethnic heritage of America. Cinco de Mayo has the universal appeal of victory over great odds—a triumph with which we can all identify.

Activities

1. Read and report about the courageous Cesar Chavez, the Mexican-American leader and spokesperson for the poor. Chavez, the son of migrant farm laborers, rose to leadership in the 1960's through his commitment to improve working conditions for migrant laborers through nonviolent means. Why did his efforts mean so much to so many people?

2. Mexican cookery warms the heart and soul. How many dishes can you think of that Anglos owe to south of the border cuisine? (tamales, enchiladas, tortillas, burritos, chili, salsa, Caesar salad) With help from the class, make a mouthwatering list. Attach an adjective to every dish—as in tempting tortillas, snappy salsa, rich refried beans.

GA1153

56. Cinco de Mayo

Fifth of May

A special time
There is no doubt
Our independence
Is what it's about.

A wonderful day
The fifth of May
All of our neighbors
Can party today.

Dance to the rhythm
Marimba beat
Flamboyant costumes
Fast moving feet.

Warming to springtime
Alive to the sweet
Festival revelry
Holiday treats.

Listen to speeches
Explaining this day
Cinco de Mayo
The fifth of May!

Greta B. Lipson

Lesson 57: Mother's Day

Since the days of antiquity, sons and daughters have expressed their love and respect for their mothers. In medieval England, young people who worked as servants and apprentices were permitted to go home only once a year on Sunday to visit their mothers. The day was called Mothering Sunday, and gifts of sweet cakes and primroses were carried home as a token of love on this day that so many cherished. In America, Mother's Day is observed on the second Sunday in May. This day was established by official proclamation of President Wilson in 1914. Anna Jarvis, a schoolteacher, is recognized as the founder of Mother's Day. She worked tirelessly to establish a day which she felt would give people a proper sense of reverence and respect for the person who had nurtured them. It was her idea that such an observance would help spread goodness and kindness into other areas of people's lives. There is a special Mother's Day stamp issued in 1934, which has inscribed on it, "In Memory and in Honor of Mothers of America." On the stamp is the famous picture, *Whistler's Mother*, which was changed to include a bowl of carnations which were the favorite flowers of Anna's mother. In her mother's memory, Anna introduced the custom of wearing a red carnation in honor of Mother, and a white one in remembrance. Mother's Day is observed by children in countries all over the world—some on different dates perhaps, but in much the same way, with heartfelt expressions of love and tenderness.

Activities

1. You can make your own personalized Mother's Day greeting card which is fun and easy to produce. Choose a piece of colorful construction paper 8½" x 11". Fold it in half. On the front cover draw a large coffee cup with signs of steam rising from the coffee. Leave room for a plastic spoon to be glued at the side of the cup. Next you will need a sugar cube. Glue the sugar cube into the bowl of the plastic spoon. Now glue the spoon next to the coffee cup. Inside the folded greeting card use the poem on the following page, "Today You Don't Need Sugar!" You may duplicate it or copy it in your own writing. We guarantee your card will get rave reviews! Add designs as you wish.

2. Make a written plan for things you could do for your mother that would make her special day sweet as sugar. Be realistic and imaginative about what you and your family can manage.

57. Mother's Day

Today You Don't Need Sugar!

Today you don't need sugar,
I really want to say!
My love will sweeten everything
You touch on Mother's Day.

Greta B. Lipson

115   GA1153

Lesson 58: Memorial Day

On this holiday, dating back to 1868—post Civil War, we pay our respects to the men and women who gave their lives in the service of our country. It is the day on which Americans decorate the graves of fallen soldiers. The tragic casualties of the Civil War, the Spanish-American War, World Wars I and II, the Korean War, and the Vietnam War are reminders that the most significant way to honor soldiers in the long history of wars is to teach for peace. To observe this day, locate the book *Shrapnel in the Heart: Letters and Remembrances from the Vietnam Veteran's Memorial* by Laura Palmer (Random House, Inc., 1987). Have students read these letters aloud in an eloquent and compelling tribute. The following letter attached to the Memorial Wall was written by a nurse who went to Vietnam in 1966 for two tours of duty*. She worked in an evacuation hospital which was an emergency facility where the wounded were brought in from the field. In that place— the horror, the pain and the impact of war was at its most grotesque.

Hello, David—my name is Dusty.
I'm your night nurse.
I will stay with you.
I will check your vitals
*   every 15 minutes.*
I will document
*   inevitability.*
I will hang more blood
*   and give you something*
*   for your pain.*
I will stay with you
*   and I will touch your face.*

Yes, of course,
*   I will write your mother*
*   and tell her you were brave.*
I will write your mother
*   and tell her how much you loved her.*
I will write your mother
*   and tell her to give your bratty kid sister*
*   a big kiss and hug.*
What I will not tell her
*   is that you were wasted.*

I will stay with you
*   and I will hold your hand.*
I will stay with you
*   and watch your life*
*   flow through my fingers*
*   into my soul.*
I will stay with you
*   until you stay with me.*

Goodbye, David—my name is Dusty.
I'm the last person
*   you will see.*
I'm the last person
*   you will touch.*
I'm the last person
*   who will love you.*

So long, David—my name is Dusty.
David—who will give me something
*   for my pain?*

---

*From *Shrapnel in the Heart* by Laura Palmer. Copyright ©1987 by Laura Palmer. Reprinted by permission of Random House, Inc.

58. Memorial Day

Thank You on Memorial Day

Do you hear us
In your deathly repose?
We've come to say thank you.
You have your country's gratitude.

Your lives,
Barely begun—now finished.
How much better,
Had they not been spent.

I'm not sure—
Tell me
How do we thank young men,
Fed into the mouth of a grave?
How do we thank young men
For giving up their lives?

Tell the families who loved them,
The reasons why it had to be.
Be sure to be convincing.

But first—
Remind us again . . .
What was the cause?
What was the war?
Where was the place?
Did we keep the peace?

Greta B. Lipson

117

GA1153

Lesson 59: World Environment Day

Environment Day has been observed annually since 1976. It was established in Stockholm, Sweden, at a U.N. Conference on the Human Environment. The purpose of this day is to educate people to their responsibility toward our endangered world. Nobody owns nature! And nobody has the right to destroy nature. The planet Earth is in a struggle for survival because of what humans are doing to it. Our seas are awash with suffocating algae, and there is dangerous ultra violet radiation due to ozone depletion. We are witnessing the destruction of tropical rain forests*, faced with global warming and threatened by the desecration of the land from mining, timber and oil interests. The hazards to the environment must be addressed by all people everywhere in the world. It is imperative to educate and dedicate ourselves to the causes of clean air and water, wise land use and energy conservation. There are groups that have been organized to actively protect the environment. One of the oldest of these organizations is the Sierra Club, which started the movement for conservation in 1892 and now conducts an International Assembly in an attempt to establish an "environmental ethic here and around the world."

Activities

1. An American child strains the ecosystem thirty times greater than one born in poorer countries. To understand your considerable personal use of energy, chart your energy consumption on a typical day—from morning to night. Example: Turn on lights, hot shower, morning radio, electric stove, toaster . . .

2. What can you do, as a family, in the battle against pollution? Example: Help to recycle bottles and newspapers. Write to the Sierra Club for a free copy of the newsletter "Somebody Do Something," Sierra Club, 530 Bush St., San Francisco, CA 94108. You can also write to the U.S. Environmental Protection Agency, Washington, D.C., for the booklet "Our Endangered World."

---

*Rain forests are being destroyed at the rate of 77,000 acres per day. More than one half of the world's animals and plants inhabit these forests. From the World Wildlife Fund, 1250 24th St., N.W., Washington, D.C. 20037.

59. World Environment Day

Save the Planet

E is for the *environment* of our precious threatened planet.

A is for *all* of earth's creatures large and small
   who must be cherished and protected.

R is for *respect* for nature's wondrous gifts
   which support life on our planet.

T is for *teaching* the world-family about the interdependence
   of nature's resources—our fountainhead.

H is for *helping* the survival of earth's treasures now—
   and for the hope of future generations.

Greta B. Lipson

GA1153

Lesson 60: Flag Day

Flag Day, June 14, is a time of national observance when the flag is flown from homes and public buildings all over the country. Though Flag Day is not a national holiday, it marks the date in 1777 when the Continental Congress adopted this banner as our national flag. There is a legend that a flag maker named Betsy Ross designed our first flag, but historians are not sure of the accuracy of this story. Our flag is sometimes called the Stars and Stripes. The alternate red and white stripes are set off by the five-pointed stars, each of which represents one of the fifty states. Each color of the flag has a special meaning. Red represents the hardiness and courage of our nation; blue symbolizes justice, vigilance and perseverance; and white emphasizes the purity and innocence of newfound liberty. Old Glory is the proudest symbol of our nation, and there are many rules related to the ways in which people display and honor the flag. It is interesting to note that the largest flag in the United States belonged to the J.L. Hudson Company in Detroit. It was 235 x 104 feet and covered seven stories of the Hudson Department Store. It was flown for the last time June 14, 1976, and was then sent to the Smithsonian Institution in Washington, D.C.

Activities

1. Have a debate or a discussion regarding the following issue: On June 21, 1989, the Supreme Court ruled that burning the flag as a political protest is protected expression under the First Amendment to the Constitution, which guarantees freedom of religion, speech and the press. The House and Senate approved a resolution denouncing that decision. President George Bush said he would propose a constitutional amendment to outlaw flag burning.

    • Some people believe that flag burning is a desecration of what our flag symbolizes.
    • Some people believe that the Bill of Rights, the first ten amendments to the Constitution, has served our nation brilliantly for two centuries without change and should not be altered.
    • Some people believe that flag burning, though crude, is a legitimate means of political expression.

2. What do you think about this issue? Listen to all opinions expressed in class. Express your own opinion in a paragraph or a newspaper editorial.

 GA1153

60. Flag Day

Banner Bright

The next time you see
Old Glory go by
Hail to its majesty
Long may it fly.

We take from this source
Its historical force
With all that implies
As it flutters on high.

The flag raises emotion
Engenders devotion
Its hues emblematic
In terms democratic.

The red, white and blue of it
All that is true of it
Compressed in our symbol
Old Glory on high!

Greta B. Lipson

121

GA1153

Lesson 61: Summer Sun

June 20 or 21 is the first day of summer—the longest day of the year—the day when the glorious sun rises at 5:57 a.m. and sets at 9:13 p.m. The daylight hours on this day total 15 hours and 20 minutes. Check the weather section of your daily newspaper for that information and more. The light and heat from the sun is the source of life for all growing things and from the beginning of humankind has been an object of mystery and deification. Even today we speak of people who spend hours tanning themselves as "sun worshippers," which brings us to the fact that the sun must be respected, for it can be very harmful to skin and eyes. The sun is the center of a huge system of heavenly bodies that revolves around it. Included in the sun's family are planets, planetoids, moons, comets and meteors. The earth is the third planet from the sun—which is 93 million miles away from us. The sun is like a giant atomic furnace with heat and light waves radiating from its surface and is sometimes called our daytime star. The stars we see at night are distant suns that seem to twinkle, because they are so very far away. The sun appears to rise in the east and set in the west. Day and night on our planet are caused by the rotation of the earth on its axis as it revolves around the sun. When our part of the earth faces the sun, it is daylight; when we are turned away from the sun, it is night. It takes the earth one year to complete one revolution around the sun. Without the sun's light and heat, life on earth could not exist.

Activities

1. For creative people in the fine arts, the sun has long been a metaphor because it is a powerful life force in our existence. To understand the sun's formidable might, read the Greek myth "Phaethon." It is the story of the twelve-year-old child of the sun god Apollo. The boy wanted desperately to prove something to his school friends and found himself in fatal trouble! Does that sound familiar? How would you have avoided a similar mess?

2. "It rises in the east, you know, and sets down in the west . . . ." The sun is a dependable direction finder. If you can admit the truth, tell a story of getting turned around and hopelessly lost because you couldn't get your bearings. There is now hope for people who have relied haltingly on paper maps. The electronic map is being produced which fits on the dashboard of commercial and passenger vehicles. What are the advantages?

122

GA1153

61. Summer Sun

Rise East—Set West

My world revolves around you,
Glorious orb
Celestial topaz.

I proclaim my intoxication
With your welcome visitation,
Radiant yellow sphere.

I come to you in the clutch of
Unremitting cold
—Grab me fast
In your hold.

After months of gray and overcast—
Enraptured by your felicity
To my world.

I cherish your
Unwavering promise
That you will come
To those of us who wait.

It would appear
You come to me
From heaven's gate.

(But now we must add
A cautionary notion
Protect yourselves
With sun screen lotion!)

Greta B. Lipson

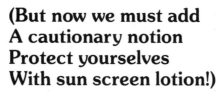

GA1153

Lesson 62: Father's Day

The observance of Father's Day was started in 1910 by Mrs. John Bruce Dodd in Spokane, Washington. She felt deeply that fathers should have a day of respect and appreciation from their children. In 1924 President Coolidge recommended that this special day be observed nationally. Children in the United States and Canada honor their fathers with gifts and cards on the third Sunday in June. Any day that is set aside to say "thank you" is especially important for the giver and the receiver both. Father's Day is the time to let your father, grandfather, uncle, older brother or guardian know how much you appreciate him as your friend and protector. The official flower on Father's Day is a red rose for the living and a white rose in memoriam.

Activities

1. Write a paragraph with an appropriate title of your choice: "A Special Person" or "A Wonderful Dad" or "My Hero" or "Gramps the Great." Write about all of the things that make your selectee such a fine person. Make this a character study that comes to life for the reader.

2. Make a Father's Day card that looks like a shirt front. Fold a piece of construction paper in half. Trim the front as if it were a shirt. Glue on some buttons, cut out a necktie or a bow tie to be glued on. Make the shirt striped or polka-dotted, as fancy as you wish! Paste the poem inside the card (see the following page).

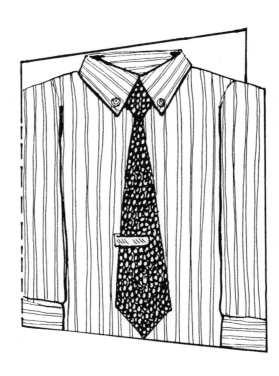

124

GA1153

62. Father's Day

A Declaration of Praise

If you want to express
Some special praise
To Dad (or Gramps)
Who won't be fazed
You can cluster your words
In a meaningful way
To express how you feel
On Father's Day.

Put these together
For your edification
Using your own inclination
To share your personal interpretation

As follows:

fair-square
impart-heart
teach-reach
tower-power
bright-delight
understands-hands
talk-walk
build-thrilled
forget-fret
years-dears
kind-mind
smile-mile
glad-sad
clever-endeavor
pleasure-treasure
swing-sing
test-best
despair-grey hair
proud-crowd
love-above
true-you

Greta B. Lipson

GA1153

Lesson 63: National Hot Dog Month

Something there is that loves a hot dog! Americans eat hot dogs in restaurants, at home, on city streets, at the beach and all over the place because they are so delicious! We owe our lust for the hot dog to the wave of German immigrants who came to this country in the 1880's and brought their wonderful sausages with them—frankfurters, bratwurst, liverwurst, weisswurst and lots more. It is not hard to figure out that the home of the frankfurter was Frankfurt, Germany, where franks were born in 1852. It was a short trip from a naked frankfurter—to a hot dog nestled in a toasted bun. The honors for the invention of the bun go to two men: Antoine Feuchtwanger in St. Louis in the 1880's and (ten years later) equally to Charles Feltman, a pushcart peddler. Feltman was in business at the seaside resort, Coney Island, New York, when he expanded his enterprise and opened a stand. His grillman, Nathan Handwerker, who was earning $11 a week, finally opened up his own stand. The rest is history. Nathan went into business using his wife's recipe "Ida Handwerker's Spicy Special!" He took the advice of two steady customers— a couple of small time performers (Jimmy Durante and Eddie Cantor)— and lowered the ten cent price. That hot dog stand grew to be "Nathan's Famous," one of the most illustrious enterprises in the world, where you could buy a hot dog smothered in mustard and sauerkraut for only a nickel! Every style of hot dog sandwich has its aficionados across the country, but the special combination in Detroit is worthy of mention. In the early 1900's Greek immigrants opened up a restaurant called Lafayette Coney Island on Lafayette Street. Their dogs were smothered with hot chili, mustard, and onions! In 1964 the Coneys were introduced to the Detroit suburbs by Bill Lipson and sold under the sign of "Athens Coney Island," where the legend on the window reads, "Tables for Ladies." (The sponsor of National Hot Dog Month: National Hot Dog & Sausage Council, 1211 West 22nd Street, Suite 1100, Oak Brook, Illinois 60521.)

Activities

1. Identify your favorite food. What ingredients go into it? How do you think it's made? Guess if you have to. Contribute to a class cookbook with a self-explanatory title such as *Yum*. Get a favorite recipe from your parents or relatives. Bring it to school to duplicate and share. Don't be afraid of spicing the book with humor.

2. Take turns reading aloud from the following hilarious food books for little kids: *Smashed Potatoes* by Jane G. Martel, Houghton Mifflin, 1974; *Eats* by Arnold Adoff, Lothrop, 1979; *Cloudy with a Chance of Meatballs* by Judith Barrett, Athenium, 1978.

63. National Hot Dog Month

Hot Dog!

I yearn for a dog
Hot off the grill
Cooked to a turn
For a red hot thrill.

Sizzle and sear
That crimson skin
Look out stomach
It's coming in.

Hungry, quivering
Upper lip
Spread that mustard
Tip to tip.

Ketchup, onions,
Sloppy chili
Sometimes even
Piccalilli.

Watch those tasty juices run
Ease into a super bun.

Greta B. Lipson

GA1153

Lesson 64: Literacy Day

Illiteracy poses a serious threat to a democratic society which requires an informed citizenry to function effectively. With Senate Joint Resolution 304, the Congress has designated July 2 as National Literacy Day. "This observance is intended to increase awareness and encourage participation in the fight for literacy in our land." The dimensions of this problem are cited by Jonathan Kozol in *Illiterate America* (New American Library, 1985), where he states that nearly 25 million Americans are nonreaders and another 35 to 40 million read below ninth-grade level. In the book *American Renaissance*, by Cetron & Davies (St. Martin's Press, 1989), the authors note that one million high school students drop out every year and another 700,000 are barely able to read the diplomas they receive from high school.

In 1989 the First Lady, Barbara Bush, had a major literacy foundation named after her in which programs were launched to teach reading skills to school children and their parents. Research indicates that the reading proficiency of parents affects children's reading achievement "more than income or race." The foundation aims to establish family literacy centers with the commitment of community, corporations, volunteers and financial support for all phases of development. The example of Cuba and its successful tutorial campaign against illiteracy is most often cited in research when, in 1969, Cuba closed its schools for a year and sent teachers and older students to tutor in rural areas. The illiteracy rate was reduced from 25 percent to about 4 percent in that reading immersion effort. Volunteer reading tutors can and do make a difference wherever they may be!

Activities

1. Organize a group of volunteers from your classroom to tutor lower elementary students who have reading problems. Make arrangements with the help of your teacher. Get a firsthand experience with the dynamics of reading. The United Nations Educational, Scientific, and Cultural Organization (UNESCO) has also designated a day in September as International Literacy Day, but you can help someone read on any day.

2. A homophone is a word that has the same pronunciation as another word (which may or may not be spelled the same). The context of the sentence gives the clue to which homophones have been used incorrectly, but the reader must have adequate reading skills to make a decision. Brainstorm a list of homophones; then create your own Phoney Homophone Story. For example:

   It was knight time and the hoarse and eye were happy four the fare whether. Hour trip started in the mourning when the son was high in the blew sky. We new their mite bee reign buy ate o'clock!

64. Literacy Day

Ode (Owed) to Literacy

Take these 26 wonderful, incredible,
Mysterious letters in the alphabet
And build a code.

Then make words from the letters
And phrases from the words
And sentences and thoughts and feelings
And moods and ideas and concepts.

Then share the written words—from the writer to the reader.
Share the thoughts,
The written prose and poetry
With anyone who wants
   Or needs them.
Build grand things with the words
Like science and literature, and art and justice and hope and
The meaning of life
And history and the future
And wisdom and philosophy.

Build words for the heart, the soul and the senses—side by side.

All that from 26 wonderful, incredible, symbolic letters?

Naah!
Can't be!
I don't believe it!
Tell me something that doesn't strain credulity!

(Credulity: A tendency to believe too readily; easily convinced)

Greta B. Lipson

Lesson 65: Independence Day

Independence Day is one of America's most significant and glorious holidays. It commemorates the signing of the Declaration of Independence by John Hancock, president of the Continental Congress, on July 4, 1776. This momentous event took place in Philadelphia, where the document was unanimously adopted by the delegates of the thirteen colonies. It is most interesting to note that, at first, the colonists did not consider independence! This was emphasized earlier by Thomas Jefferson who stated that he "sincerely" would rather be dependent upon Great Britain than any other country in the world. It was a great leap, from that expressed political position, to the document which was primarily written by Thomas Jefferson, who was among the youngest and most articulate of the revolutionary leaders. The observance of July 4 was carried on throughout the years and by 1880 it had become a major occasion shared by patriotic Americans who celebrated with hoopla, fireworks and pride all over the nation.

Activities

1. On July 8, 1825, when Thomas Jefferson was an old man, he reflected on the design of the Declaration of Independence. He wrote a letter to a friend, Richard Henry Lee, in which he said that his task had been ". . . not merely to say things which had never been said before . . . nor yet copied from any particular and previous writing. It was intended to be an expression of the American mind." Have a class reading of the eloquent document which is titled "The Unanimous Declaration of the Thirteen States of America":

   "When in the Course of human events it becomes necessary for one people to dissolve the political bands which have connected them with another, and to assume among the Powers of the earth, the separate and equal station to which the Laws of Nature and of Nature's God entitle them, a decent respect to the opinions of mankind requires that they should declare the causes which impel them to the Separation.

   We hold these truths to be self-evident, that all men are created equal, that they are endowed by their Creator with certain unalienable Rights, that among these are Life, Liberty and the pursuit of Happiness.—That to secure these rights, Governments are instituted among Men, deriving their just Powers from the consent of the governed.—That whenever any Form of Government becomes destructive of these ends, it is the Right of the People to alter or to abolish it, and to institute new Government, . . ."

GA1153

65. Independence Day

Independence Day Acrostic

Flag unfurled to honor
Our day of independence
Under this symbolic banner
Ready to celebrate
The signing of the Declaration of Independence by John
Hancock, and fifty-five others!

One nation, indivisible, with liberty and justice
For all

Joined together by the bonds of history
United people throughout the
Land—celebrating our freedom and liberty
Yearly!

Greta B. Lipson

GA1153

Lesson 66: Summer Ethnic Festivals

The word *ethnic* derives from the Greek word *ethos* meaning "nation or people." An ethnic group is made up of people who share the same national origin and who may be of the same race and religion. They share a particular culture, language, history and background. One may add or subtract from the list, but it must always include a common and distinctive tradition shared by the group. Racial similarity does not, of itself, describe an ethnic group. We, in America, are either Native Americans or overwhelmingly a nation of immigrants from other lands. The notion of the "melting pot" has been eclipsed by the new wave of pride and curiosity about our different beginnings. A more appropriate description for America is to call it a "pluralistic society." In acknowledgement of this, there is a need for developing pride in ethnic heritage. From this new awareness, one is better able to reach out toward others and appreciate the unique contributions to the quality of life which come from all of us. The diversity of custom, geography, language and the arts in each ethnic group yields a rich human tapestry. This mixture of nationalities is intriguing to explore at any of the numerous summer ethnic festivals held in communities from coast to coast. These colorful gatherings, which always abound in savory foods, offer the opportunity to enjoy the folk traditions of people in an informal and fun-filled atmosphere.*

Activities

1. What is your favorite ethnic celebration? Think of an ethnic custom, ritual, tradition or game observed in your family, which you could explain to the class. What questions do you have about other ethnic groups? Do you know what a *quincerano* is for a Mexican girl? What is Mardi Gras in New Orleans? How is the Italian game of Mora played? How did American Indians play Lacrosse? What is the Moslem holiday of Ramadan? What is the name of the pre-Lenten Polish jelly doughnuts? What is a Bar/ Bas Mitzvah for thirteen-year-old Jewish children?

2. If there was one country you would like to visit, which one would it be? (You may want to visit your family's ancestral homeland.) How far is it? What would the airfare cost? What would you especially want to see there? Do your research and report back to the class. Are the airfare and distance astonishing?

---

*Greta B. Lipson and Jane A. Romatowski, *Ethnic Pride* (Carthage, Illinois, Good Apple, Inc., 1983).

GA1153

66. Summer Ethnic Festivals

Ethnic Gourmand

Wrap me in a grape leaf
Crunch me with chitlins
Tickle me with tortillas
Cool me with vichyssoise
Warm me with Welsh rarebit

Ply me with pita bread
Seduce me with a pizza
Brighten me with beet borscht
Coax me with a curry
Bombard me with baklava

Taunt me with a trifle
Fire me with Szechuan
Pep me with paprikash
Beguile me with weiner schnitzel
Tempt me with teriyaki

Goad me with gefilte fish
Hound me with haggis
Console me with corn pudding
Josh me with yummy jambalaya

Now—soothe me with a sparkling seltzer,
   please!*

Greta B. Lipson

*Plain carbonated water

GA1153

Lesson 67: National Clown Week

The Clowns of America, Inc., are the sponsors of National Clown Week, during which time they want to call attention to the wholesome entertainment and good works of clowns. Today's men and women clowns are descendants of Maccus, the favorite clown of ancient Rome, and the court jesters who entertained kings down through the centuries. P.T. Barnum, the great American showman, said "Clowns are pegs to hang circuses on." In modern times there are two basic types of clowns. The oldest type is the white-faced clown, whose makeup was devised in Paris in the 17th century by a French baker turned comedian. With the white face is worn all manner of bright harlequin costumes. The second type, and more recent, is the August clown who looks like a shabby, sad-faced hobo. The most famous August clown in America was Emmett Kelly, who was known as "Willy the Tramp." Clowns do not all look alike. Each tries very hard to make an original face. Clowns cannot copyright their faces legally, but there exists a professional agreement among them, that no clown will copy another clown's funny face. Clowns are called "joeys" by circus people, and their dressing area is called "clown alley." The circus clowns are sent out to entertain the spectators with fast and funny antics while the props are set in place during the time interlude between the big acts. One of the rules of clowning is that one must start out doing something that looks serious, but finish by doing something quite ridiculous. In addition to circus work, clowns would like to be known as messengers of cheer for their work with children, the ill and the elderly. A clown's funny pantomime, without a word spoken, can do wonders for a doleful spirit.

Activities

1. To laugh is a wonderful experience, and so there is a plentitude of synonyms for the word *laugh*. As a class activity, each person must come up with a sentence using a variation of the word *laugh*. Use any tense. When you have run out of ideas, consult your thesaurus for more suggestions such as *chortle, giggle, titter, guffaw.*

2. Originally, American clowns were talking and singing comedians, but with the advent of three-ring circuses, their style changed to straight pantomime. Try a pantomime performance with a small group of classmates. Brainstorm some themes to act out. List the ideas on the board and select one with good possibilities. Each group will rehearse and present. Suggestions: "Lonesome at the Dance," "The Show-Off," "Trouble with the Teacher."

GA1153

67. National Clown Week

A Clown to Call My Own

When I was little
I was afraid of clowns.
And my mother said,
"See all the other children laugh
And clap and exclaim?
Here come the clowns!
There's nothing here
To frighten you."

But I was still afraid
Of the stark white face,
The flaming bulbous nose,
The strange circle around
A lipless mouth,
The matted orange hair.

I covered my eyes behind my hands
Wishing them to go away.

Then I saw him
This quiet little clown
A gentle fragile soul
He moved in my direction.

He seemed to search for a familiar face
In that enormous tent
When our eyes met
He saw my outstretched hand.

Our fingers barely touched
In tender understanding
So moved was I—
I knew at once
That I had found a clown
To call my own.

Greta B. Lipson

GA1153

Lesson 68: Umpire Appreciation Day

It must be difficult to be in a vocation that generates such hard feelings! The sponsor of Umpire Day, Guy Garraghan in Windham, New York, understands the bad times and abuse suffered by umpires. So Guy suggests that we extend the milk of human kindness to these poor maligned souls and for a brief day make them feel appreciated. Hats off to the men and women who, from sandlot to professional ball, contribute to the game as umpires. Please, hug an ump on August 13! Another side of all of this is that umpires are involved in one of the most loved sports in America, where baseball is known as the "national pastime." There is, however, an unresolved item about the beginnings of baseball. Abner Doubleday was purported to be the originator of the game in Cooperstown, New York, in 1839 where the Baseball Hall of Fame resides. Obversely, historians claim that the game originated with the British game of Rounders in the 1600's which was later played by the American colonists in the 1700's. But the truth is that when we are at the old ball game and we hear the umpire say, "Play ball!" we are deeply unaffected by this historical dilemma!

Activities

1. For the time of your life, have a class reading of "Casey at the Bat" by Ernest Thayer. This classic poem ends:

   Oh! somewhere in this favored land the sun is shining bright,
   The band is playing somewhere, and somewhere hearts are light,
   And somewhere men are laughing, and somewhere children shout;
   But there is no joy in Mudville—mighty Casey has struck out.

2. Write an impressionistic, nonrhyming poem about baseball. Brainstorm colorful words and phrases that characterize baseball. Record all the ideas on the board or on your paper: power hitters, sluggers' row, jammed bleachers, hot dog fiends, kill the umpire . . . . Select the most colorful words and phrases and arrange them in a pleasing order. The final poem must have about ten lines. Your impressionistic poem might look like this for starts:

   America's passion
   Baseball
   Hometown heroes—sluggers' row
   Sunburned bleacherites
   Hot dogs, peanuts, popcorn
   Hoarse shouting—wild fans
   Strike, foul ball,
   Kill the umpire.

136

68. Umpire Appreciation Day

Hug an Ump!

That's the umpire with the rugged face
He's pretty well-known around our place
His power here is very great
'Cause his word in the game has the final weight!

And when you hear the players moan
It's because he stands on his very own.

He's been known to make grown men cry
You'll see it someday just as I.
When he calls the plays he decides your fate
And often incurs your venomous hate!

But he's fair and his honesty is high as the sky
When he watches the ball as the batters try.
And we know, though a team gets pulled apart,
He'll make his decision with a purist's heart.

You may choose to call him by a different name
But not one person can deny his fame.
So on August 13 before the game
Go out and hug this very same
                    Umpire!

Greta B. Lipson

137

GA1153

Lesson 69: Soapbox Derby Day

The second Saturday in August, 1987, marked the fiftieth anniversary of the All-American Soapbox Derby Race, held in Akron, Ohio. It all started in the early 1930's when a journalist, Myron Scott, was sent on a photographic assignment to cover a story about boys who had built their own nonmotorized cars for racing. Scott was so impressed that he copyrighted the idea in 1934 and promoted the program on a national scale! The event started in Dayton, Ohio, but moved to Akron where the hilly terrain was better for the downhill competition. The permanent track site is called Derby Downs. Here, girls and boys ages 9-16 come from all over the United States and throughout the world to race, after winning competitions in their own communities. The cars have evolved from the original soapbox cars to today's sophisticated models which are built according to regulation rules for sturdy construction. The big event in Akron lasts for four exciting days and is capped with awards of trophies, gifts and scholarships.

Activities

1. Design and/or describe the car of your dreams. Be true to yourself and don't be intimidated by anyone else's taste. ("My dream is a big Marathon taxicab, yellow and black, which is built like a fortress!") If you design a one-of-a-kind model, you must give it a name. Discuss the psychology of automobile names and advertisements. What are your conclusions after reviewing the ads?

2. For the teacher: For more information, request a few booklets for your class. Write to: All-American Soapbox Derby, P.O. Box 7233, Akron, Ohio 44306, or call (216) 733-8723. When the class receives the Derby Rule Book, the students can discuss it with their homeroom teacher or their industrial arts teacher. Is there a chance that the class could build a soapbox derby car just for the thrill of it? It could be a multi-curriculum enterprise in which every student participates.

GA1153

69. Soapbox Derby Day

Rev 'Em Up!

Senior Speedstar, Junior Jetstar
Body shell
Axles
Vertical kingpin
Brake lever
Fiberglass nose
Headrest
Steering wheel
Cockpit
Body hatch cover

Can you believe it?
Can you believe that I put it together?
That polished pointed body, sleek black,
Like a cat ready to spring.
All power and sinew.

Snug down into the cockpit
With nerves of steel
I'll race it.

Wish me well, Lady Luck!

Greta B. Lipson

GA1153

Lesson 70: Joe Miller Joke Day (1684-1738)

We doff our hats to Joe Miller on his birthday, August 16, because he was—sort of—the father of the centuries old *Joe Miller Joke Book*. Miller was an English actor who performed with the Drury Lane Company from 1709 until his death. He was distinguished as a very famous comedian who made a comic hit out of the plays of his time, most notably those of William Congreve. After Miller's death, his contemporary, John Mottley, published a collection of jokes named *Joe Miller's Jest Book*, later changed to ". . .Joke Book." In truth, it was later revealed that Miller had told only three of the jokes contained in that coarse compendium. Somehow Miller's name has come down in history as being synonymous with any book that is a collection of yaks. It could be that the laugh is on us because there is no longer a *Joe Miller Joke Book* to be found in print! (If you can locate one, let us know.) But who cares! What really matters is the glorious tradition of humor that lightens our burdens and gives us great belly laughs. So, wherever you are Joe or Joseph or Josias Miller—we are eternally grateful for your legacy.

Activities

1. Everyone will contribute to a class joke book entitled *It's a Funny Thing About Humor*. Search for a funny, appropriate joke to tell the class. (Ethnic jokes are off limits!) Write the joke in its entirety, which will give you a chance to become familiar with it. Keep the joke easy and well-timed for telling. All jokes will be handed to the teacher for inclusion in the class book. On an appointed day, be courageous and tell your joke. Insist that the teacher tell a joke, too! Rehearse at home for a smooth delivery.

2. A Joke: The schoolmaster, Mr. Puckett, was expecting a visit from his superintendent, whom he knew to be a pious man. Puckett told his pupils that the superintendent would ask them one important question—"Who made you?" Anxious to make an impression, Mr. Puckett rehearsed little Oscar in the correct answer—"God made me." On the appointed day all went smoothly in class until the superintendent finally asked the question: "Who made you?" He waited but no one answered. He asked again. No one answered. Finally, one little girl raised her hand and broke the silence, "Sir," she said, "the boy God made is absent today!"

For a funny read-aloud activity, locate *The Ring Lardner Reader* by Maxwell Geismer, Scribners, © 1963.

70. Joe Miller Joke Day

The Joker's Disciple

He's the joker of the class
A shrimp with lots of sass
A mouth aflap that opens at both ends.

The teacher warns this clown
"The next time—you'll go down
To the office where
They're waiting for your act."

In a second of a stroke
He makes another joke
Strutting like a chicken
Pecking seeds.

Eyes fix upon her face
'Cause he's fallen from her grace
The punishment will come now
Swift and sure.

She's lost all her control
The comic's on a roll,
The laughter bounces off
From wall to wall.

The teacher is his captive
As she gives into the rapture
Of the deep dismaying talent
Of this clown!

Greta B. Lipson

141

Coming Events
September

School Starts

Labor Day

The Four Seasons

Autumn (Official Autumn, September 22 or 23)

Banned Books Week

Native American Indian Day

Pickled Pepper Week

Coming Events
October

National Popcorn Poppin' Month

Columbus Day

Migration of Birds

Statue of Liberty Birthday

Halloween Witch

Halloween Cat

Halloween Owl

Halloween Mask

GA1153

Coming Events
November

Invention of the Sandwich

Basketball Founder's Birthday

Thanksgiving Guests

Thanksgiving Menu

Coming Events
December

Hanukkah

Winter Holiday (Official Winter, December 21 or 22)

Christmas Santa

Christmas Angel

Christmas Tree

Kwanzaa

National Whiner's Day

GA1153

Coming Events
January

New Year's Day

Martin Luther King, Jr.'s, Birthday

Chinese New Year

Snowflakes

The Common Cold

Coming Events
February

Black History Month

Groundhog Day

Thomas Edison's Birthday

National Inventor's Day

Abraham Lincoln's Birthday

Valentine's Day

Susan B. Anthony's Birthday

George Washington's Birthday

Leap Year

Coming Events
March

Women's History Month

March Weather (Official Spring, March 20 or 21)

Alexander Graham Bell's Birthday

Albert Einstein's Birthday

Anniversary U.S. Standard Time Act

Kite Festivals

Saint Patrick's Day

Maple Sugar Time

Coming Events
April

April Fool's Day

Easter Rabbit

Easter Eggs

Spring Rain

Arbor Day

GA1153

Coming Events
May

Law Day

May Day

Cinco de Mayo

Mother's Day

Memorial Day

Coming Events
June

World Environment Day

Flag Day

Summer Sun (Official Summer, June 20 or 21)

Father's Day

GA1153

Coming Events
July

National Hot Dog Month

Literacy Day

Independence Day

Summer Ethnic Festivals

Coming Events
August

National Clown Week

Umpire Appreciation Day

Soapbox Derby Day

Joe Miller Joke Day

Bibliography

(This is a practical list of basic books consulted in the construction of this book. It does not include the books footnoted in the text.)

Bernardo, Stephanie. *Ethnic Almanac*. New York: Doubleday & Co. Inc., 1981.

Birnbaum, Hollis, et al. *Official International Directory of Special Events and Festivals*. Chicago: 1984.

Chambers, Robert. *Book of Days*. Detroit: (republished) Gale Research, 1967.

Chase, W.D. and Helen M. *Chase's Annual Events*. New York: Contemporary Books, 1988.

Cohen, H. and T.P. Coffin, Editors. *Folklore of American Holidays*. Detroit: Gale Research, 1987.

Gregory, Ruth W. *Anniversaries and Holidays*. Chicago: American Library Association, 1983.

Harelson, Randy. *Amazing Days*. New York: Workman Publishing, 1979.

Hatch, Jane M. *American Book of Days*. New York: The H.W. Wilson Company, 1978.

Hill, Kathleen T. *Festivals U.S.A.* New York: John Wiley Sons, Inc., 1988.

Koek, K.E., S.B. Martin, et al., Editors. *Encyclopedia of Associations*. Vol. I-II. 23rd Edition. Detroit: Gale Research, 1989.

Lipson, Greta B. and Jane A. Romatowski. *Ethnic Pride*. Carthage, Illinois: Good Apple, Inc., 1983.

Urdang, L. and C.N. Donohue, Editors. *Holidays & Anniversaries of the World*. Detroit: Gale Research, 1985.

World Book Encyclopedia. Chicago: World Book, Inc.,—A Scott Fetzer Company, 1988.

Index of Lessons

GA1153

GA1153

GA1153

GA1153